Understanding
RAVENNA

Understanding
RAVENNA

MICHAEL STARKS

FONTHILL

Fonthill Media Language Policy

Fonthill Media publishes in the international English language market. One language edition is published worldwide. As there are minor differences in spelling and presentation, especially with regard to American English and British English, a policy is necessary to define which form of English to use. The Fonthill Policy is to use the form of English native to the author. Michael Starks was born and educated in the UK; therefore, British English has been adopted in this publication.

Fonthill Media Limited
Fonthill Media LLC
www.fonthill.media
books@fonthill.media

First published in the United Kingdom and the United States of America 2018
Reprinted 2024

British Library Cataloguing in Publication Data:
A catalogue record for this book is available from the British Library

Copyright © Michael Starks 2018, 2024

ISBN 978-1-78155-711-2

Typeset in 10pt on 13pt Sabon
Printed and bound in England

Contents

Preface

All visitors to Ravenna marvel at the city's eight early Christian churches and monuments, recognised as World Heritage sites by UNESCO (United Nations Educational, Scientific, and Cultural Organisation). Surviving from the fifth and sixth centuries are three churches, three chapels or mausoleums, and two baptisteries. Their finest feature is their interior decoration in wonderful Roman and Byzantine mosaics.

I too admired their beauty and charm. Then I became very curious about how such rich art and architecture could have been created in Ravenna in the era when the Roman Empire was disintegrating all around (we conventionally date the fall of the Roman Empire from AD 476 when the last Western emperor was deposed). Why Ravenna and how in those circumstances? I wanted to understand as well as admire. It was that curiosity that prompted this book.

It is not a guidebook to the eight UNESCO monuments. There are plenty of guidebooks and plenty of serious art books too. My aim is to explain the historical context of the buildings and the mosaics to provide a broader understanding and add to the visitor's appreciation. This is not a book for specialist scholars, though I hope that those who teach will find it an introduction to the subject that they can recommend. Essentially, it has been written for general readers of ancient history, for students of all ages, and for visitors and would-be visitors to Ravenna.

The book is organised very simply. Chapter 1 poses my question of how and why Ravenna's uniquely rich and well-preserved monuments were built and painstakingly decorated during such a chaotic and often destructive era. It recounts the importance of mosaics in early Christian art, briefly describes each of the UNESCO monuments, and gives a picture of the invasions, civil strife, and war damage that characterised the fifth and sixth centuries.

Chapter 2 sets out three themes that start to answer the question, each of which forms a motif running through the narrative history which follows. Chapter 3 addresses the question of 'Why Ravenna?' by telling the 'backstory' of the Roman Empire, its external threats, and its changes of capital city prior to the fifth century. Chapter 4 then covers the fall of the Western Roman Empire and brings in the two UNESCO monuments from this period in their historical context. Chapter 5 describes the rule of Italy by the Ostrogoths and the four monuments created under their regime. Chapter 6 recounts the reconquest of Italy under the Eastern Roman Emperor Justinian and the completion and decoration of Ravenna's two major churches during his reign.

Chapter 7 then offers a concluding answer, drawing together and augmenting the three themes established earlier before addressing the further question of how these eight monuments survived until today when so many other early Christian monuments, elsewhere but even here too, did not.

I conclude with suggestions for further reading. Specifically on Ravenna, Deborah Mauskopf Deliyannis's *Ravenna in Late Antiquity* provides an authoritative academic study. Mariëtte Verhoeven's *The Early Christian Monuments of Ravenna* presents an architectural history, covering later modifications to the buildings as well as their original forms. Salvatore Consentino has charted Ravenna's transition from 'imperial residence to episcopal city'. Then Judith Herrin and Jinty Nelson have edited *Ravenna: Its Role in Earlier Medieval Change and Exchange*, which offers a number of fresh insights into the Late Antiquity period and, importantly, looks beyond it to later centuries. The range of books I have listed on the Late Roman Empire, Byzantium, early Christian Art, and the Goths covers the wider picture. The Notes indicate ways in which I have drawn on them and I gratefully acknowledge a debt to them all.

I am especially grateful to Professor Judith Herrin for giving me access to the text of her lecture *Why Ravenna*, given at the University of Utrecht in September 2016 as part of the Heineken Prize ceremony, and for her further generous help and advice. Her assessment of the evidence for the location and character of the imperial and regal palaces of Ravenna was much appreciated.

I am also grateful for the help of Dr Werner de Saeger of the University of Brussels, whose seminar lecture on Ravenna I attended in Oxford, and for the insights I gained from the Continuing Education courses in Oxford taught by Dr Aphrodite Papayianni of Birkbeck College, University of London, and Richard Massey of Cotswold Archaeology. I have also drawn on John McNeill's 2017 lecture on San Vitale to the London Art History Society.

I would like to thank Mark Phythian-Adams warmly for his constructively critical reading of an early draft of the book and for pointing me towards relevant scholarship. I am grateful to Dr Allan Doig for reading my draft text on the early history of church design and decoration. I also thank Anna di Stefano for linguistic assistance, Susan Starks for her editorial expertise and advice, Alison Davies of the Mapping Company for the maps, and Aline Ramond of UNESCO for permission to use Aneta Ribarska's copyright pictures. I would like to give special thanks to Dr Vitaliana Pantini and Dr Giada Ravaioli of the Municipality (*Comune*) of Ravenna for the use of photographs and for their generous assistance more widely; I also appreciated help from Professor Giovanni Gardini and Dr Maria Vittoria Maioli in Ravenna.

I have used the term 'barbarians', as the Romans did, to refer to peoples beyond the frontiers of the Roman Empire. No slur on the ancestors of northern Europeans, or anyone else, is implied. I have also used the term 'orthodox Catholic Church' when I want to distinguish its doctrines from various early Christian heresies. This is partly as a reminder that, although a formal schism developed much later, the orthodox Church and the Catholic Church formed a single body during the fifth and sixth centuries. There were disputes and stand-offs between Constantinople and Rome, but so there were, for example, between Constantinople and Alexandria.

I have adopted a pragmatic approach in presenting the names of emperors, kings, saints, and churches, opting for the form that seems to be in widest use, and therefore mixing English, Latin, Italian, and different ways of anglicising Greek and Persian names. This should help the reader make connections with other works. I have used generally recognised dates but must caution that dates for births and deaths and for the foundation and completion of buildings are not always known precisely. Any mistakes are my responsibility.

Michael Starks

Outline Chronology

395: Division of the Roman Empire into East and West
402: Ravenna becomes the 'capital' (imperial residence) of the Western Roman Empire
410: Sack of Rome by Alaric the Goth
452: Attila the Hun's invasion of Italy
455: Sack of Rome by the Vandals
476: Last Western emperor, Romulus Augustus, deposed by Odoacer
493: Odoacer killed by Theodoric the Ostrogoth who then rules Italy
526: Death of Theodoric
527: Justinian becomes Eastern Roman (Byzantine) emperor
540: Initial reconquest of Italy by Justinian's general Belisarius
542: War in Italy revived by the Ostrogoths
552: Final defeat of the Ostrogoths by the Byzantines
565: Death of Justinian
568: Lombards invade Italy; Ravenna remains a Byzantine outpost

Beauty in the Twilight of the Roman Empire

Ravenna is a small city in north-east Italy, south of the marshy Po delta and today, several miles inland from the sea, with a population of around 160,000. It sits in flat countryside devoted to agriculture, fruit orchards, and light industry. To a visitor arriving by train from Bologna, it may at first look unprepossessing but a walk into the old city with its ancient walls, narrow cobbled streets, brick churches, cylindrical bell towers, and palace-flanked piazzas gives an early insight into its remarkable past.

In the fifth and sixth centuries AD, Ravenna was an imperial and regal capital city within the crumbling Western Roman Empire. At that time, it was on the sea with its harbour to the south of its city walls in a deep lagoon. The first emperor, Augustus, chose it as Rome's naval base for the Adriatic and it is said to have sheltered a fleet of 250 ships. The harbour area developed into the separate port district of Classe (from *classis*, Latin for 'fleet').[1] Criss-crossed by waterways stemming from its marshy surroundings and lapped by the Adriatic, Ravenna became the centre of a thriving commercial trade, linking Italy to Africa and to the Eastern Roman Empire. Today, the old port of Classe is an inland archaeological site. Its ancient warehouses, and traces of the goods they once stored, have been recently excavated and the site is now open to tourists.

In medieval times, the sea receded from Ravenna and it was displaced as a major maritime centre by Venice. Indeed, Ravenna was ruled by the Venetian Republic during the fifteenth century. The *Piazza del Popolo* at the centre of the old city today preserves a Venetian look, but the early Christian heritage is also evident here.

The arcade of the *Palazzetto Veneziano* stands on six granite columns whose capitals came from a sixth-century church. In front of the adjacent town hall are two columns surmounted by statues. One is of St Apollinaris (Sant'Apollinare), believed to have come from Antioch to Rome and been sent to Ravenna as its first bishop, where he was arrested, tortured, and killed during a first-century persecution of Christians. The second is of St Vitalis (San Vitale), who is said to have travelled from Milan to Ravenna and been buried under stones in a pit during a second-century persecution. Both figures are legendary, with more than one version to their legends (and St Vitalis

Above: Ravenna's *Piazza del Popolo* and town hall. (*Delio Mancini*)

Below: Map of modern Ravenna and the Adriatic.

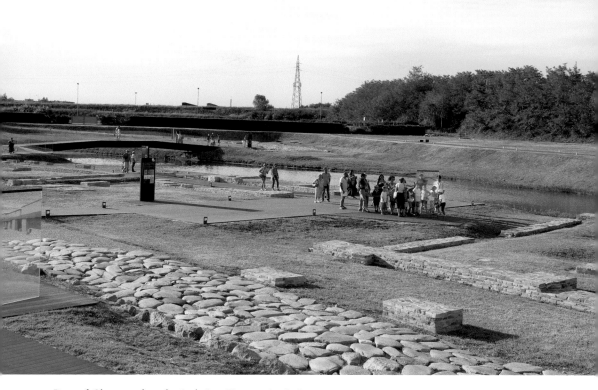

Port of Classe archaeological site. (*RavennAntica*)

is thought to have been appropriated from Bologna), but they became Ravenna's patron saints and gave their names to its finest sixth century churches: Sant'Apollinare Nuovo and Sant'Apollinare in Classe and San Vitale.[2]

It is the splendour of Ravenna's late Roman art and architecture—and especially the mosaic decoration—that attracts visitors here now. UNESCO has listed eight of Ravenna's monuments as World Heritage sites. People who have been to Sicily and admired the twelfth-century mosaics in the royal chapel in the Norman palace in Palermo and the cathedral of Monreale catch their breath as they realise that Ravenna's are some 600 years older. Ravenna is home to some of the finest art and architecture of the period we now call Late Antiquity.

The eight UNESCO sites comprise three churches, two baptisteries, two chapels (one of which is termed a mausoleum), and a standalone stone tower, which is also a mausoleum. Visitors can visit all eight sites over one or two days. They are nearly all close together.[3] Ravenna's Tourist Office offers the free use of bright yellow bicycles for visiting them and the one distant site, Sant'Apollinare in Classe, is easily reached by bus. Seen together, they evoke both the early Christian era and the interplay between religious architecture and imperial rule.

St Apollinaris. (*Author's collection*)

St Vitalis. (*Author's collection*)

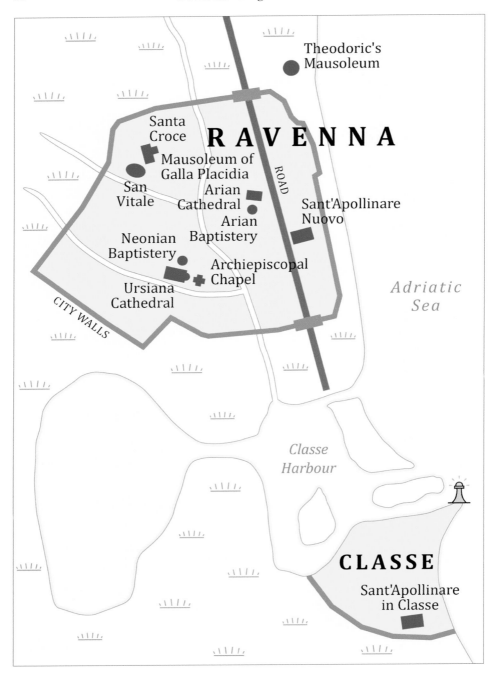

Theodoric's Mausoleum

Santa Croce

R A V E N N A

Mausoleum of Galla Placidia

ROAD

San Vitale

Arian Cathedral

Sant'Apollinare Nuovo

Arian Baptistery

Neonian Baptistery

Archiepiscopal Chapel

Ursiana Cathedral

CITY WALLS

Adriatic Sea

Classe Harbour

C L A S S E

Sant'Apollinare in Classe

Sketch map of ancient Ravenna, *c.* AD 550, showing the eight UNESCO sites and adjacent buildings (though Sant'Apollinare Nuovo did not then have its present name).

The Eight Sites

The eight UNESCO sites are listed here briefly and described more fully individually in later chapters in their historical context.

The oldest is the Mausoleum of Galla Placidia, a small cross-shaped brick building with exquisite interior mosaic decorations of flowers and stars against dark backgrounds and vivid religious scenes. Galla Placidia was the sister of one Roman emperor and the mother of another. She may have commissioned this chapel as an oratory rather than a mausoleum. Its original purpose is uncertain.

From the same period, before the fall of the Western Empire, comes the Neonian Baptistery, an octagonal building originally linked to an adjacent cathedral. It is named after Bishop Neon of Ravenna (episcopacy 450–473) who transformed and redecorated it. Its mosaic portrayal of the baptism of Christ in the Jordan River is the centrepiece of a richly decorated dome.

The next four buildings were constructed under the rule of the Ostrogoths, whose King Theodoric reigned here from 493 to 526. The Ostrogoths were Arian Christians. The Arian heresy is explained in more detail in the next chapter but essentially the Arians held that Christ was not as fully divine (not of the same substance) as God. The Goths built their own cathedral and attached to it was the Arian Baptistery with a simpler representation of Christ's baptism in the Jordan.

Theodoric's palace has now disappeared but next to its supposed location stands the Ostrogoths' greatest church: Sant'Apollinare Nuovo. This is a long basilica with magnificent mosaic decorations in three tiers along its walls. These have an important history: some are still the Gothic originals, but others were replaced after Emperor Justinian reconquered Italy from the Ostrogoths when the church was reconsecrated to orthodoxy.

During the Ostrogoth period, the orthodox Catholics continued to build and Bishop Peter II of Ravenna (episcopacy 494–520) constructed the Archiepiscopal Chapel for the private use of the bishops. It too has some fine mosaic decoration and is now part of an Archiepiscopal museum occupying the bishop's palace.

Theodoric's Mausoleum is a splendid two-storey stone tower built outside Ravenna's city walls. His body was removed long ago, but a porphyry sarcophagus in the shape of a bath on the upper floor is said to have once contained it.

Ravenna was reconquered from the Ostrogoths by Justinian's general Belisarius in 540. By then, two major orthodox Catholic churches had been founded and were consecrated by Bishop Maximian (episcopacy 546–557) whom Justinian promoted to archbishop.

Seeing San Vitale is the high point of a visit to Ravenna. An intricate octagonal shape in design, with soaring columns emphasising its height, it has a sanctuary bright in colour and rich in mosaic scenes and images. At the far end of the sanctuary is an equally sumptuous apse with a semi-dome that groups Christ, two angels, St Vitalis, and Bishop Ecclesius (who founded the church). On the side walls of the sanctuary are group portraits featuring Emperor Justinian, together with Archbishop Maximian, and the Empress Theodora.

Above: Mausoleum of Galla Placidia. (*JIPEN/Shutterstock.com*)

Below: Neonian Baptistery (*Dmytro Surkov/Shutterstock.com*)

Above: Arian Baptistery. (*Michal Szymanski/Shutterstock.com*)

Below: Sant'Apollinare Nuovo. (*UNESCO/copyright Aneta Ribarska*)

Theodoric's Mausoleum. (*Author's collection*)

Above: Archiepiscopal Chapel. (*Opera di Religione della Diocesi di Ravenna*)

Below: San Vitale. (*JIPEN/Shutterstock.com*)

Sant'Apollinare in Classe, nave. (*UNESCO/copyright Aneta Ribarska*)

Some 5 miles south of Ravenna, near the old port, lies Sant'Apollinare in Classe. Like Sant'Apollinare Nuovo, it is a large basilica to which a tall, round, bell tower was later added. It can be seen from afar across the flat countryside between Ravenna and Classe. At the east end of its nave, a triumphal arch forms a gateway into a beautifully decorated pastoral scene in the apse. At its centre, below a large cross, stands St Apollinaris.

Church-Building

Our modern focus on the eight UNESCO sites should not lead us to think that they stood alone. They are just the ones that survived most successfully, either in their original form or something close to it. In the fifth and sixth centuries, Ravenna enjoyed a major programme of church-building. With Christianity now the official state religion of the Roman Empire, the social and political pressure on pagans to convert was strong and the growing number of converts drove the demand for additional churches and for baptisteries.

With a population of perhaps 10,000 at its height, Ravenna is thought to have had more than fifty churches.[4] Many of these are known to us, including St Euphemia, St Lawrence Caesarea, San Giovanni Evangelista, Santa Croce, San Francesco (originally the Church of the Apostles), Sant'Agata Maggiore, the Ursiana Cathedral, the Arian Cathedral (Santo Spirito), St Severinus, San Michele in Africisco, Santa Maria Maggiore, St Stephen, St Andrew, Saints John and Paul, and St Victor. These are just churches in Ravenna itself; many more were built in Classe. Some have disappeared completely and are known only from written records; in other cases, early structures were incorporated into, or replaced by, very different designs in a later era.

When the early Christians were at risk of persecution, their private houses formed the basis for simple churches. A well-known and relatively well-preserved example of a *domus ecclesiae* (house-church) has been excavated at Dura-Europos on Syria's eastern border. When public worship first developed, however, church design had to be invented. Pagan temples did not provide a model; they usually housed a shrine of some kind at which the priests officiated, leaving the mass of worshippers outside, often in front of the steps where the sacrificial altar was sited. Christians wanted an indoor place of worship that would bring the priest, the altar, and the congregation together. They adopted—and adapted—the basilica design from Roman secular architecture.

The church-building in Rome instituted by the first Christian emperor, Constantine, set the pattern. The Lateran Basilica was his first foundation in the early fourth century. It was rectangular in shape with a plain exterior. A high central hall formed the nave which was separated by long colonnades from the lower aisles. At the east end, behind the altar, was a semi-circular apse with a semi-dome. Outside stood a separate baptistery. The basilica design forms the basis of Ravenna's Sant'Apollinare Nuovo and Sant'Apollinare in Classe.

Constantine's church of St Peter in Rome (demolished in the sixteenth century) introduced a transept at the east end, making a T-shape, and this concept evolved later into the conventional Latin Cross pattern of western churches, with a long nave crossed by a shorter transept. A common form in early Christian architecture, however, is the Greek Cross, with arms of equal length and a dome over the crossing. Entry could be through an entrance hall (or narthex). The Mausoleum of Galla Placidia and the Archiepiscopal Chapel in Ravenna are cross-shaped.

Two other traditional Roman architectural features were carried over into early Christian buildings: the domed rotunda and the octagon. Theodoric's mausoleum in Ravenna is a domed round tower, while the octagon shape was adopted for the Neonian and Arian baptisteries and, in a much more elaborate form, for San Vitale.

Church Mosaic Art

Interior church decoration also had roots in secular Roman tradition. Mosaic art had a history in the Middle East and particularly in ancient Greece before permeating the pagan Roman Empire. Elaborately detailed mosaic floors, built up with thousands of tiny pieces of stone (*tesserae*), became a feature of grand Roman villas. The patterns were often geometric but also included representations of plants, animals, fish, and pastoral scenes with figures. Examples can be seen today in the *Domus dei Tappeti di Pietra* (House of the Carpets of Stone) museum in Ravenna. The Great Palace Mosaic Museum in Istanbul has some wonderful examples, though perhaps the finest display is in the fourth-century Roman villa at Piazza Armerina in Sicily, another UNESCO World Heritage site. The use of the tessellated technique spread from floors to walls and was developed in dramatic new ways in early Christian art.[5]

Christian artists used mosaics to create an aura of religious awe and splendour, and also to illustrate episodes from the Bible for congregations, often illiterate, for whom art and images constituted a primary medium of communication. Large-scale mosaic compositions were made up of thousands of glass or stone *tesserae* incorporating bright colours, gold especially, and placed so as to catch and reflect the light.

Craftsmen worked like painters to create distinctive facial features, shadows, and patterns and folds of garments to represent scenes from the Bible. The images could be pictorially literal: the naked Christ being baptised in the Jordan River seen both above and through the water, for example. Old and New Testament stories were told, martyrs remembered, and saints revered. As the art form matured, symbolic representation became established, using codes in which congregations were literate. The four Gospels were portrayed by four symbolic figures: a man representing St Matthew, an eagle St John, a lion St Mark, and an ox St Luke. Then, especially in vaulted ceilings and domes, the artists created star-studded skies and visions of angels and heaven.

Pictorial mosaic art (on walls, in apses, over vaults, and in domes) was a feature of early Christian art in a wide range of places, most obviously in Constantinople (where most of it was subsequently destroyed) and in Rome as at Santa Maria Maggiore. Famous examples can be found in Thessalonica's round church of St George (formerly the Rotunda of Galerius), in Milan's chapel of St Aquilino in the Basilica of San Lorenzo, and in St Catherine's monastery in Sinai. However, their concentration, their state of preservation, and their artistry make the mosaics of Ravenna quite exceptional.

The Question

As the grandeur and beauty of Ravenna's early Christian heritage sinks in during a visit, a fundamental question arises: how did such a magnificent array of buildings and decorative art come to be constructed here at that time? The scale of the buildings, and of the many others that have disappeared, arose from a commitment over decades, and the individual mosaic displays were pieced together over years. They must have been created in a social environment marked by civic stability and wealth. Yet those are not characteristics we associate with the years between AD 400 and 600. This was the period of 'the Decline and Fall of the Roman Empire'.

Care needs to be taken in using that familiar phrase. First of all, the Fall was only of the western half of the empire: the Eastern Empire survived in shape-shifting form until the fifteenth century. Second, when the last emperor in the West, Romulus Augustulus, was deposed in 476, the Western Roman world did not suddenly collapse: imperial authority had already been eroded by then and there was significant administrative continuity thereafter. Nonetheless, we can say that the period during which Ravenna's finest monuments were being constructed was characterised by external attacks, political disintegration, periodic civil war, economic weakness, and turbulence.

The heart of the problem was that the Western Empire lost the ability to defend itself effectively. The causes have been the subject of much scholarly debate. Were the external threats which the empire had faced for centuries now that much greater? Could internal decay be held responsible? Had there been economic decline? If so, when did it start and how widespread was it? Historians will continue to argue over these questions.

Whatever the balance between external and internal factors, in the course of the fifth century, invasions and rebellions lopped outer provinces off the empire and dramatically reduced its tax base. The majority of tax income was spent on military defence, so the loss of revenue weakened the army and, in a vicious circle, made the empire more vulnerable to invasion. Moreover, devastated regions had to be granted temporary tax relief because of the economic damage inflicted by marauding invaders. Emperors who failed to defend the empire successfully were challenged by usurpers. So Roman armies who might otherwise have been repelling invaders instead fought other Roman armies who were supporting rebels. Barbarian incursions increased, imperial rule crumbled and, by the end of the fifth century, the outer western provinces had been lost and Italy was ruled by a Gothic king.

Major Italian cities were therefore recurrently besieged and invaded. Alaric the Goth invaded Italy in 401 and besieged Milan before being driven off. In 407, after another group of Goths had attacked in the meantime, he returned and penetrated deep into Italy. The Romans paid him a huge ransom, which they only raised by stripping temple artworks in Rome. However, Alaric soon returned again, first blockading Rome and then in 410 famously sacking the city. The next major invader was Attila the Hun, who attacked Milan in 451. He did not get as far as Rome but the Vandals did. They sacked the city in 455. In 489, the Ostrogoths arrived and laid siege to Ravenna for three years before establishing their rule over Italy.

In the sixth century, Eastern Emperor Justinian attempted to expel the Goths from Italy, precipitating two decades of destructive civil war. Led by Belisarius, the imperial invaders captured Sicily in 535 and then took Naples after a siege. Belisarius was welcomed into Rome but besieged there by the Goths for more than a year. In 539, the Goths sacked Milan and slaughtered the adult male population.

Throughout this prolonged period of fighting, other cities were besieged and captured, the countryside devastated, and the economy fractured. The imperial victory of 540 proved temporary. The Ostrogoths renewed the war and besieged Rome in 546. When they occupied it, they expelled most of its remaining citizens and then withdrew. Belisarius reoccupied it, so the Goths returned to subject the city to its third siege, capturing it again in 550. Imperial forces finally recaptured Rome and defeated the Ostrogoths conclusively in the early 550s, but Italy by then was almost a wasteland. Then in 568, the Lombards invaded and by 600 controlled two-thirds of the country.

This short account, of course, gives a very incomplete picture of the Western Roman Empire and its successor regimes over the course of 200 years but it clearly underlines the point that this was not an era of stability and prosperity.

A cameo of the first half of the fifth century is provided by the individual experience of Galla Placidia, the sister of Western Emperor Honorius whose so-called Mausoleum is the earliest of Ravenna's UNESCO sites. She was kidnapped by the Goths during the sack of Rome in 410. She was then married to one of the Goth leaders, by whom she had a son who died. She was later returned to the Romans and remarried to the Roman General Flavius Constantius, by whom she had a son and a daughter. Constantius became co-emperor and Galla Placidia thus an empress. Soon afterwards, however, Constantius died, as did her brother, Emperor Honorius, in 423. Galla Placidia then had to defend the claim to the throne of her infant son against a usurper. She succeeded, and her son reigned as Valentinian III until he was murdered in 455. Meanwhile, his unhappily married sister, Honoria, Galla Placidia's daughter, had intrigued with Attila the Hun, allowing him to claim she had offered him marriage and using this, so it is believed, as a pretext for invading Italy.

In this political and military climate, how could Ravenna's architectural and decorative arts have flourished so splendidly?

Searching for the Answer

In answering the question, sources of help are, of course, the evidence of the extant buildings and archaeological work on the sites of ruined churches and palaces. The site of the ancient harbour of Classe, now inland, continues to be excavated. There are some relevant written records too.

Theodoric the Ostrogoth employed the Roman statesman Cassiodorus in his administration in a series of political roles and Cassiodorus's collection of state papers, the *Variae Epistolae*, has survived as a source for historians. Cassiodorus also wrote a history of the Goths that has been lost but which was used as a source in the *Gothic History (Getica)* of Jordanes, a monk of Gothic parentage writing in Constantinople around 550. Both writers were admirers of Theodoric.

Justinian's reconquest was chronicled by the contemporary historian Procopius, who accompanied Belisarius on his military campaigns and wrote a series of books on Justinian's wars. He also wrote in praise of Justinian's building programme of churches and aqueducts. Then, amazingly, during the seventeenth century, a *Secret*

History of Justinian's reign by Procopius was discovered in the Vatican library: it provides a disillusioned and rather scurrilous portrait of the emperor and his empress, Theodora.

On Ravenna specifically, an important source is the ninth century local historian, Agnellus, a priest and author of the *Book of Pontiffs of the Church of Ravenna*. This gives biographies of the city's bishops from the earliest known through to Agnellus's own time. It is from this source that we know of early Christian churches in Ravenna that have now disappeared or been largely rebuilt.

Then, of course, there is the huge body of work by modern historians of the fall of Rome and its aftermath, from Edward Gibbon onward, drawing on the full range of ancient authors, secular and Christian, and on still-emerging archaeological evidence. As we shall see in the next chapter, their interpretations of the period have changed significantly within the last generation.

Three Strands of Continuity

Historians' Debates

Our traditional preconceptions of the fall of the Roman Empire can be traced back to Edward Gibbon's famous six-volume work, *The History of the Decline and Fall of the Roman Empire*, published in 1776. Few of us may have read it in full, we do not always recall that he placed the final fall in the fifteenth century when Constantinople was conquered by the Ottoman Turks, but we have inherited the picture he gives of a decline from the 'full strength and maturity' of the second century empire of Trajan and the Antonines, through the 'subversion of the Western Empire by the barbarians of Germany and Scythia' to the culmination of an 'extraordinary revolution which subjected Rome to the power of a Gothic conqueror' around the beginning of the sixth century.[1]

We inherited the idea of a world divided into civilised Romans and uncouth, backward and warlike barbarians, with the latter winning out when the last Western Roman emperor was deposed in AD 476. Gibbon ascribed the Western Empire's fall to a range of causes but at heart, he believed that the Romans lost their ability to combat barbarian invasions through decadence and an inability to defend themselves militarily, attributable in part to the malign influence of Christianity. He bequeathed us a focus on the empire's political, military, and institutional history, with its unedifying saga of dissolute and incompetent emperors, over-mighty imperial guards, upstart generals, usurpers, and barbarian invaders interrupted by the occasional statesman or military hero trying to stem the tide of decline.

These assumptions shaped the work of historians who continue to debate the range and relative weighting of all the possible contributory causes (for details of the modern historians' works mentioned here, see Further Reading). For example, Michael Grant, invited to re-examine the subject for the 200th anniversary of Gibbon's publication, argued that the invasions were not sufficiently formidable by themselves to have caused the Western Empire to fall; he identified thirteen internal flaws that in combination prevented the Western Empire from effectively defending itself. These include conflicts between the generals and the state, between the people

Edward Gibbon (1737–1794), engraving by William Holl. (*Georgios Kollidas/Shutterstock.com*)

and the army, between the people and the state, between the Eastern and Western halves of the empire, as well as between the Romans and the German barbarians. He also cites the impact of Christianity, whose monks, nuns, and hermits opted out of society, and whose Church leaders looked to spiritual salvation in the next world rather than military salvation in this.

However, modern historians have opened up another level of debate altogether. Instead of asking why the Western Empire declined and fell, they have challenged our inherited ideas more fundamentally by asking whether it actually declined and fell at all. We should not picture the period simplistically as one of incessant destructive warfare in which invaders brought a high civilisation to an abrupt end and plunged Europe into the gloom of semi-barbarism. The period of history after 476 was not that different from the period before. The Romans and the Goths were not as separate, or as different, from one another as we have tended to assume.

A seminal work here is Peter Brown's 1971 book, *The World of Late Antiquity*. He challenged the mental construct of an era that ended in the late fifth century. Instead, he pictures an era of Late Antiquity spanning the years AD 200 to 800. This concept places less emphasis on political and institutional history and more on social and cultural changes and trends, especially on the shift from polytheistic paganism to the monotheistic religions of Christianity, Judaism, and Islam. Christian Romans and Christian Goths had a cultural affinity with one another that differentiated their world from that of ancient history. Brown narrated his history from the third to the ninth century without portraying decay or catastrophe, describing instead a religious and cultural revolution.[2]

Another key revisionist figure was Walter Goffart who in 1980 published *Barbarians and Romans 418–584: Techniques of Accommodation*. His argument was that the concept of barbarian invasion itself needed to be re-examined. We should picture the Goths as would-be settlers, migrants and asylum seekers, whom the Romans agreed to try and integrate into the empire. His most provocative assertion was that 'what we call the Fall of the Western Roman Empire was an imaginative experiment that got a little out of hand'.[3]

An important corrective to revisionist historians who emphasised continuity was then provided by Bryan Ward-Perkins's 2005 study, *The Fall of Rome and the End of Civilisation*. Challenging the unfashionability of talking about a decline or collapse of civilisation leading to the Dark Ages, he makes the case that there was indeed a startling decline of living standards in western Europe between the fifth and the seventh centuries, which contrasted with the experience of the Eastern Empire. It was often violent and painful and involved a loss of comfort, convenience and skills at all levels of society. Roads and aqueducts fell into disrepair. Classical learning was lost. While the Goths, Franks, and others may have been able to craft jewellery on an occasional basis, the Romans had the complex manufacturing and distribution skills needed to produce a range of good quality low value goods, pottery in particular, for day-to-day living in households generally. The barbarians did not intend to destroy the economic sophistication of the Western Roman Empire (they just wanted their own place within it), but over time, they did destroy it.[4]

However, in the revisionist interpretations of Brown and Goffart, we can find two themes that help explain how Ravenna created such glorious art and architecture while the Western Empire crumbled: first, the role of the Church in providing continuity and development through this politically and militarily disrupted period, and second, the complex and nuanced relationships between the Romans and the Goths.

The Church and the Empire

The Church's relationship with the empire went through a series of transformations. Initially, when Christians worshipped in their own largely private groups, they had been subject to sporadic bouts of persecution. Emperor Nero was held to have blamed them for the great fire of Rome in AD 64. Generally, Rome's polytheistic paganism supported a high degree of religious toleration, but the Christians' main offence was to insist that theirs was the only God. Further persecutions occurred under Domitian, Trajan, and Marcus Aurelius. Decius was the first to implement an organised empire-wide persecution in 250. He issued an edict requiring all citizens to perform a sacrifice, under supervision, to Rome's pagan gods and those who refused could be executed. This was targeted in practice at the monotheistic Christians (the monotheistic Jews, as they did not proselytise, were exempt). Valerian (253–260) too ordered the execution of recalcitrant Christians but persecution proved counter-productive, as underground Christian organisations defiantly developed a cult of martyrs.

The Roman Empire then began to move towards a pagan form of monotheism. Emperor Aurelian (270–275) adopted the oriental worship of the Unconquered Sun (*Sol Invictus*) and elevated it into the state religion, with a central role for himself. Deification of emperors (and even of some imperial family members) had started back in the first century AD and Aurelian now portrayed himself as an emanation of his chosen deity. His great successor, Diocletian (284–305), presented himself as god-like. Few were allowed to come near him and those that did had to prostrate themselves. The Christian God who excluded all others was a threat to the imperial quasi-divinity. Diocletian initiated a ruthless persecution of Christians.

It was Constantine (306–337) who dramatically transformed the relationship. In 312, having ordered his troops to paint a Greek Christian symbol on their shields, he famously defeated his rival Maxentius in the Battle of Milvian Bridge and attributed his victory to the support of the Christian God. He gave Christianity formal recognition and acceptance within the empire and ordered the restitution of property seized from Christians during the persecutions. He also lent Christianity his own personal support, partly in deference to his mother Helena, who was a fervent Christian. Constantine himself did not formally convert until, perhaps, on his deathbed, but he regarded himself as Christ's Regent on earth. After the brief reversion to paganism of Julian the Apostate (361–363), all succeeding emperors adopted Christianity and Theodosius (379–395) made it the official state religion. Christianity became coterminous with the Roman Empire and even spread beyond.

The emperors quickly inserted themselves into this new increasingly dominant religion. Christian emperors could not, of course, be gods but they could become God's secular representatives on Earth. Emperors convened and presided over Ecumenical Councils to address theological disputes. They used Christianity to buttress their own authority and legitimacy. Constantine himself was a great church builder, funding the construction of St John in Lateran and St Peter's in Rome as well as the great Church of the Holy Apostles in his new capital of Constantinople. Imperial church-building was for the glorification of God but, not unintentionally, for the emperors' glorification as well. Roman emperors thus became patrons of Christian architecture. The main imperial supporter of Ravenna's fifth-century church-building was Galla Placidia, sister of Emperor Honorius and mother of Valentinian III. Her Mausoleum commemorates her name, though it does not house her body.

However, while Roman emperors adopted Christianity, Christians were more ambivalent about adopting the Roman Empire. They were reluctant to fight for it. Christianity was not spread by soldiers in the way that Islam would be later. It spread initially through example, teaching and persuasion. Many Roman Christians turned inward to monasticism. At the end of the third century, St Anthony, who gave up his worldly goods and became a hermit, inspired many followers to live an ascetic semi-communal life outside the mainstream of Roman society. In the fourth century St Martin, who famously tore his cloak in two in order to give half to a beggar, was a Roman soldier who became a conscientious objector, declaring 'I am a soldier of Christ—it is not lawful for me to fight'.[5] He then lived as a hermit before later becoming bishop of Tours. Gibbon made much of the corrosive effect that Christian pacifism had on the spirit of the Roman army.

With Christianity as a favoured religion, Christians could now emerge to develop the Church as a formal organisation, led by the Pope as bishop of Rome and by Patriarchs in Antioch, Jerusalem, Alexandria, and Constantinople. Bishops who had previously led small communities of local believers now became the heads of large dioceses with a range of managerial duties covering everything from buildings and liturgy through to care for the poor and the resolution of disputes. The empire drew them into civil administration but, within the Church, they kept their own separate identity. Some of them became powerfully independent figures: Bishop Ambrose of Milan (374–397) famously forced Emperor Theodosius to do penance for a massacre he had ordered in Thessalonica.[6]

In the fifth century, as imperial rule weakened under barbarian attacks and internal strife, another transformation began. The Church in the west began to dissociate itself ideologically from the empire. After the sack of Rome in 410, St Augustine wrote *The City of God*, contrasting the imperilled earthly City and the heavenly spiritual City in which Christians should place their faith. The earthly City housed the unrighteous, dead souls, and fallen angels as well as living sinners, while the City of God encompassed angels, saints, and all who had led righteous lives on earth. Under an earthly ruler of great virtue, like Theodosius, the Roman Empire could, Augustine believed, begin to have a shadowy resemblance to the City of God, but the empire was the source of many evils. Earthly crises and catastrophes should be ignored by

Christians, or even welcomed as disciplinary punishments sent by God. God's earthly creation would come to an end: it should be no surprise if the Roman Empire did so first. Christians should instead focus on their own salvation in the eternal life hereafter.

The Church did not champion the survival of the Western Roman Empire, therefore. What it did instead was to distance itself from the imperial regime. It thus ensured that, when the Western Empire collapsed, the Church not only survived but continued to grow. The imperial treasury's resources shrank as the empire crumbled, but the Church's coffers expanded as wealthy Romans contributed to religious foundations to help ensure their own salvation. When imperial patronage of church-building declined, the Church was able to invest independently in churches and monasteries. During the last decades of the Western Empire, the Cathedral Baptistery in Ravenna, founded earlier by Bishop Ursus, was transformed by Bishop Neon, who redecorated its interior in marble and mosaic. Then, under the Ostrogoth regime of Theodoric, the bishops built the Archiepiscopal Chapel adjoining their palace.

When Italy was reconquered by the Eastern Empire in the sixth century, imperial patronage returned to Ravenna and Emperor Justinian and Empress Theodora are famously portrayed in mosaic panels on the side walls of the apse of San Vitale. However, this church and its contemporary Sant'Apollinare in Classe were essentially the work of the Church and its donors. Much of the credit belongs to Bishop Ecclesius and his successors, including Archbishop Maximian, who is prominently pictured in Justinian's mosaic panel, but it was a wealthy banker named Julian who provided the finance.

Amid the political and military upheavals associated with the fall of the Western Roman Empire, therefore, the Church managed to sustain artistic commitment and funding. Led by its bishops, it provided a vital line of continuity during the disjuncture of the successive fifth- and sixth-century regime changes.

Roman–Barbarian Relationships

A second important theme is the relationship between the barbarians, especially the Goths, and the Roman Empire. As modern historians of the fall of Rome have stressed, there were barbarians inside, as well as outside, the Roman Empire.

The term 'barbarian', derived from Greek usage, was applied to all outside Rome's frontiers but there were, of course, many different barbarian people (ranging from the Picts to the Parthians) and their relationships with the Romans varied greatly by region and over time.

The Roman Empire had initially been formed by conquest back in the era of the republic, before there were any emperors. New territory was commonly acquired through the brutal campaigns of republican generals like Marius, Sulla, Pompey, and Caesar: the king of Pergamum's decision to bequeath his kingdom to Rome in 133 BC was exceptional.

By the time of Augustus (27 BC–AD 14), the main shape of the empire had been drawn. It expanded to its greatest extent in the reign of Trajan (AD 98–117).

After a traumatic third-century crisis, it decreased with Aurelian's decision to abandon Dacia in the 270s and withdraw back across the Danube. The north-west frontier remained under frequent threat; the eastern frontier was contested, and altered, in wars with Persia; and there were periodic rebellions. For all that, however, the empire (stretching from Britain to Syria, and from Spain through North Africa to Egypt) stayed a recognisably similar shape from the early first to the early fifth century. Over this period, the empire was held together by its success in assimilation. The conquered barbarians of the republic became the civilised provincials of the empire. After Caracalla awarded citizenship to all free men within the empire's frontiers in AD 212, they became Romans.

In the context of Ravenna and the fall of the Western Empire, we are primarily concerned with the northern frontier and the Balkans. The imperial frontier lay along the strategically defensible lines of the Rhine and the Danube. Along the southern river banks were the assimilated citizens of the Roman provinces, settled in towns, villages, and farming estates, literate, bureaucratically governed, and defended by a professional army. Across the rivers on the northern side were shifting tribal groups, some literate, others not, some sedentary and others nomadic, all with strong warrior

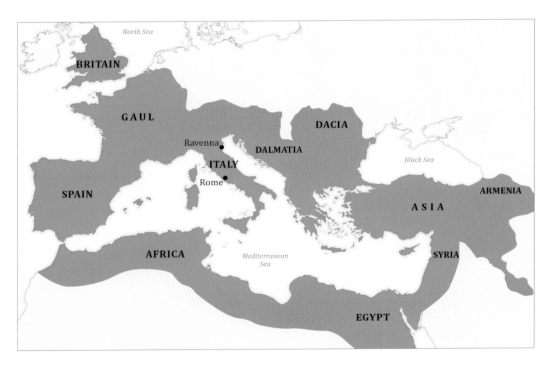

Map of the Roman Empire at its greatest extent, AD 117.

the Huns behind them or the Vandals who were to march through Spain and conquer Roman Africa. Inside many a Goth was a would-be Roman. The Romans looked down on the Goths but, politically, they developed a willingness, to a degree, to accommodate them—or, at any rate, some of them, on the right terms.

When Theodoric the Ostrogoth became king of Italy at the end of the fifth century, the relationship was reversed. The Ostrogoths, to a very substantial degree, accommodated the Romans. Theodoric founded a regime which was based in many respects on Roman foundations, was culturally compatible with Roman beliefs and institutions, and employed Romans in its service. He nurtured a nominal allegiance to the eastern emperors in Constantinople, kept on good terms with the Pope and he left the orthodox Catholic Church free to continue building its own churches.

At the same time, Theodoric stimulated the construction of places of worship for the Goths, building a cathedral with the adjoining Arian Baptistery and, next to his own palace, the Ostrogoths' greatest church, the brilliantly decorated Sant'Apollinare Nuovo. Arian church-building developed within the same architectural and artistic traditions that the Roman Christians had established, very probably using many of the same artists and craftsmen and the representation of the baptism of Christ in the cupola of the Arian Baptistery resembles the portrayal in the Neonian Baptistery.

Theodoric's Mausoleum, constructed outside the city walls in an area used by the Goths as a graveyard, is in a distinctively different style, blending Roman, Middle Eastern and Gothic elements. After his death, his daughter, acting as regent for his grandson, sought to maintain her father's regime, including good relations with Constantinople and with the orthodox Catholic Church. It was actually during this period that the construction of San Vitale and Sant'Apollinare in Classe was started.

Here then is a second strand of continuity in the historical background to Ravenna's art and architecture: after the fall of the Western Empire, a key line of continuity was provided by the semi-Romanised Ostrogoths.

Capital City

If the combination of the Church's continuing independent growth and the nuanced relationships between the Goths and the Romans could alone explain the magnificence of the art and architecture of Ravenna, then we would expect to find comparably glorious fifth and sixth century churches and monuments elsewhere in Italy and western Europe. Ravenna's heritage, however, is quite exceptional.

The third interacting element in the explanation is Ravenna's position as the capital city of the Western Empire in the fifth century. The term needs qualification: 'co-capital' with Rome is the term some historians use. Its central place in the late empire and then in the successor regimes in Italy accounts for the richness of its religious buildings.

Ravenna, though a busy naval and commercial port on the Adriatic before its coastline receded, was still a minor city by Roman standards at the start of the fifth century. Both Milan to the north-west and Aquileia, on the coast further north at the head of the Adriatic, were bigger and more important. However, in AD 402, Emperor Honorius (395–423) chose to make it the capital of the Western Roman Empire by taking up residence there.

Ravenna's appeal was largely related to its defensive position: surrounded by marshland, it was difficult for invaders to capture and, in any siege, it could be provisioned from the sea. It also had a good sea-and-land communication links to the Eastern Empire and its capital Constantinople. Rome remained the home of the Senate and retained its imperial symbolism but it was no longer the city where the emperor lived and governed. The machinery of government—the imperial bureaucracy—also moved to Ravenna therefore. Honorius's successor Valentinian III (425–455) ruled from Ravenna for twenty-five years, though he returned to Rome for the final five years of his reign. Four of the last nine emperors, whose short-lived reigns culminated in the fall of the Western Empire, also resided in Ravenna, including Romulus Augustulus who was deposed in 476.

Despite the turmoil of the barbarian raids and invasions of Italy Ravenna experienced a building boom between 402 and 476. As the imperial capital, the city needed a palace, state buildings for the Roman administrators and a mint, as well as improved defences including new city walls.

The city's imperial status was reflected in the Church: Ravenna's bishop was promoted to be a metropolitan with authority over neighbouring dioceses, overshadowing Milan which, especially under Bishop Ambrose, had previously been more prominent. A cathedral, baptistery, and episcopal palace were built. Galla Placidia supported the Church and the bishops by sponsoring further church-building.

Romulus Augustulus was deposed by Odoacer, a barbarian of Scirian descent, who made himself King of Italy. Crucially, Odoacer retained Ravenna as his capital. Ruling with the consent of the Senate in Rome and acceptance, for the time being, by the Eastern emperor, he brought a measure of stability to Italy. An Arian himself, he maintained good relations with the orthodox Catholic Church, preserving its buildings in the city.

After ruling for seventeen years, Odoacer was overthrown, at the instigation of Eastern Emperor Zeno, by Theodoric the Ostrogoth who invaded and occupied Italy as its new king. He ruled Italy from 493 until 526. He too maintained Ravenna as his capital and, as mentioned above, left the remarkable architectural legacy of the Arian Baptistery, the Basilica of Sant'Apollinare Nuovo, and his own Mausoleum. He also replaced the imperial Roman palace with his own. The palaces themselves are no longer there but an image of Theodoric's palace is preserved in a mosaic in Sant'Apollinare Nuovo.

Theodoric's Ostrogoth successors were overthrown by Eastern Emperor Justinian (527–565), who ambitiously aimed to reconquer the former Western Empire provinces of Africa and Italy to restore the Roman Empire of old and to root out the Arian heresy. When Ravenna was captured in 540, it became the capital of the Italian province of the Eastern Empire. Justinian promoted the bishops of Ravenna to archbishops and it was the most famous of these, Maximian (546–557), who oversaw the completion of San Vitale and Sant'Apollinare in Classe.

Sant'Apollinare Nuovo, the palace mosaic. (*Alvaro German Vilela/Shutterstock.com*)

War between the Ostrogoths and the East Roman invaders continued for another decade. This period was characterised by widespread fighting, sacking of cities, fragmentation of trade links, disruption to agriculture, neglect of infrastructure, and economic damage. Yet Ravenna remained in East Roman hands and was spared from destruction. After Justinian's death, his successors' hold on Italy weakened. In 568, the Lombards invaded from the north and gradually extended their control over most of the peninsula. The Eastern Empire shrank back into what we, following historians of the sixteenth century, now describe as the Byzantine empire. However, while most of Italy was abandoned, Ravenna managed to survive under Byzantine control with a shrinking hinterland until the eighth century.

The Byzantines preserved much of the heritage of the Ostrogoths. The provincial governors appointed from Constantinople moved into Theodoric's palace and were subsequently given the status of Exarchs with control of both the military and the civil administration. The orthodox Catholic Church took over the Arian church properties and converted them for orthodox worship (so a portrait of Justinian was retrofitted in Sant'Apollinare in Nuovo and may have blanked out the portrayal of Theodoric).

In the end, Ravenna had the much the same fate as the rest of western Europe but its link to the Eastern Byzantine Empire, while it lasted, delayed it. Between the beginning of the fifth century and the end of the sixth, Ravenna enjoyed leading city status. This is the third strand of continuity that helps explain Ravenna's remarkable art and architecture. During these 200 years, despite three regime changes, the city experienced sufficiently continuous status and stability to be able to develop the outstanding churches and monuments we see today.

The Broad Themes

We set out with the question of how such rich art and architecture could have been created in such turbulent times. Ravenna's history during this period was rather special. The Western Roman Empire crumbled in a number of different ways. Britain was lost first: Romano-Britons under attack from Picts, Scots, Angles, and Saxons were left to their own fate. Gaul was occupied in stages by the Visigoths, the Franks, the Burgundians, and the Alamanni. Spain fell to the Visigoths and the Suevi; Africa to the Vandals and Alans. Italy was different because of the Ostrogoth regime, and, within Italy, Ravenna was different because of its 'capital' status, because it was shielded by geography and its own defences from much of the conflict, and because it retained its link to Constantinople for so long.

Continuity was crucial. Ravenna's achievements owed much to the orthodox Catholic Church, which, as the Western Empire began its collapse, successfully established its financial independence from the secular power and retained its commitment to church-building. It owed much to the Goths' admiration for the civilisation of the Romans, Theodoric's building on behalf of the Arian church, and his continuing link to the Eastern Empire. It owed much to the city's continuing role as an imperial, then royal, and then provincial capital. Roman and Byzantine artists were able to work in a continuing tradition while empires and kingdoms rose and fell around them.

In later centuries, as the sea receded, Ravenna was overshadowed by Venice as a maritime city and indeed, for a period, it fell under Venetian rule. Once its link to Constantinople was broken, Ravenna ceased to be so politically prominent. Its importance in the fifth and sixth centuries enabled its great Christian monuments to be constructed; its subsequent relative obscurity helped preserve them for posterity.

This then in broad outline is the historical context for Ravenna's eight UNESCO sites. We can now begin to narrate the full story with these themes in mind.

The Eclipse of Rome

That Ravenna became the capital of the Western Roman Empire is rather a surprise. How did it come about?

Ravenna could never have become the capital (or 'co-capital') of the Western Empire without Rome's position having first been seriously weakened. Constantine's building of Constantinople in the fourth century is, of course, a key part of the explanation, but only part. It was a four-stage process.

Rome began to lose its imperial capital status when Diocletian (284–305) created a new imperial structure following the period known as the empire's 'third century crisis'. His reforms entailed four rulers and four or more different imperial residences close to the frontiers under threat from barbarians. Then came Constantine's elevation of his own city of residence into the New Rome of Constantinople. Next came the solidification of the division of the empire into Eastern and Western halves, with Constantinople as the eastern capital. Finally came the surprising selection of Ravenna for the seat of governance for the Western Empire.

The Third-Century Crisis

The root of the third century crisis—and indeed a fundamental flaw that remained at the heart of the empire—was that there was no firmly established rule of imperial succession. The first emperor, Augustus, had finessed the creation of his position by camouflaging it in the language of the Republic. His military title was *imperator*, but Augustus tactfully called himself merely 'Romanus Princeps' (first citizen of Rome) and showed nominal respect for the Senate. After his death, following much sinister family intrigue, the succession was settled by a form of heredity, but Nero's death brought the Julio-Claudian dynasty to an end, precipitating a civil war in AD 69 (the year of the four emperors). The victor, Vespasian, established a new Flavian dynasty, but this came to an abrupt end with the murder of Domitian in 96.

Then came a long period of relative stability during which the emperors selected their own successors and adopted them. In principle, the family connection remained,

Above left: Emperor Diocletian. (*De Agostini Picture Library/Bridgeman Images*)

Above right: Emperor Constantine. (*Lefteris Papaulakis/Shutterstock.com*)

therefore, but in practice, adoption made it possible to draw on the talents of the wider senatorial class. Succession by adoption came about because three succeeding emperors were childless and a fourth had no son, but it served the empire well during the second century. Able rulers tended to choose wisely. The last in this line was the philosopher-emperor Marcus Aurelius (161–180).

Marcus Aurelius named his adopted brother Lucius Verus as his co-ruler, giving him the title of Caesar while he was styled Augustus, but Verus died in 169. Marcus Aurelius then ruled alone until 176 when he made his teenage son Commodus co-emperor and prospective heir. This reaffirmation of the heredity principle was a critical moment (reinterpreted in the Hollywood epic *Gladiator*) since Commodus turned out to be a bloodthirsty tyrant entirely devoid of his father's conscientious commitment to the welfare of the empire.

After a reign of twelve years, Commodus was poisoned and strangled in a palace coup. His successor was a senator who came to the throne by bribing the praetorian guards and, less than three months later, was overthrown and killed by those same praetorian guards in favour of another senator who undertook to pay them more.

In place of heredity and adoption, the empire now had a third succession mechanism: senatorial auction to the praetorian guards. This precipitated a period of civil war in which Septimius Severus (193–211) emerged as victor after marching on Rome with his army from the provinces and overawing the Senate.

Severus had two sons, Caracalla and Geta, whom he made his joint heirs. He thus reaffirmed the heredity principle but recognised its fragility, reportedly advising his sons to enrich the soldiers and despise everyone else. Caracalla murdered Geta and reigned alone (211–217).[1] He was on the eastern frontier when he in turn was murdered. The army there chose an equestrian who had been involved in plotting the murder, Macrinus, as his successor and simply informed the Senate of the outcome.

Thus was born a fourth mechanism for determining the succession: army acclamation without any legitimising criteria. It could potentially happen anywhere in the empire and the candidate could potentially be of any military rank.

The collapse of principle behind the process for selecting the emperor—the ruler of the world between Scotland and Syria—predictably bred assassination and civil war. In the third century, conflict over the succession was no longer periodic: it became normal. Most rulers did not reign long before they were murdered, making an unedifying saga:

Macrinus, 217–218: defeated in a battle over the succession, then killed
Elagabalus, 218–222: murdered, succeeded by his adopted cousin
Severus Alexander, 222–235: murdered by troops supporting a usurper
Maximinus Thrax, 235–238: murdered by his own troops
Gordian III, 238–244: killed in battle with the Persians or murdered
Philip the Arab, 244–249: defeated in a battle over the succession, then killed
Decius, 249–251: killed in a battle with barbarians
Gallus, 251–253: defeated and killed in a rebellion.

During this shameful period, the role of the Senate was undermined and, with it, Rome's importance as the capital. The army, whose primary role was to defend the frontiers, became politicised and open to bribery. Roman soldiers fought Roman soldiers, sometimes with barbarian troops in support. Emperors became less preoccupied with defending the empire than with guarding their own personal safety.

Political weakness bred economic decline. Progressive devaluations of the coinage by short-sightedly greedy emperors wreaked havoc with trade and commerce. Inflation was rampant. Cities shrank in size, agriculture suffered, and, in some regions, especially those hit by plague, populations fell.

On the frontiers, serious threats mounted. In the east, the Persian Sassanids had overthrown the Parthians, founding a new empire that they began to expand by attacking the Roman provinces of Syria and Mesopotamia. The Persian King Shapur I launched a series of incursions into Roman territory. It was after battling unsuccessfully against Shapur that Gordian III was killed in 244. Meanwhile, successive bands of invaders threatened the north-west frontier: Goths, Franks, and

Marcomanni. Emperor Decius was killed in 251 fighting a tribe of Goths on the Danube. Shortly afterwards, the Marcomanni raided Italy, reaching Ravenna in 254.

Worse was to come. In 253, Shapur defeated a Roman army and captured Antioch. In 260, he undertook a major invasion of Mesopotamia. Rome at that time had joint emperors: Valerian and his son Gallienus. Valerian determined to punish the Persians and led an ill-judged campaign against Shapur. His army was outmanoeuvred and defeated, and Valerian was himself taken prisoner, remaining in humiliating captivity until his death.

The military defeat and capture of the emperor was followed by the disintegration of the empire. For a period, it was effectively split in three.

In the west, a provincial governor, Postumus, proclaimed himself emperor. All of Germania, Gaul, and later Britain and Spain supported him. He therefore founded a short-lived parallel empire (sometimes called the Gallic empire) with successors Marius, Victorinus, and Tetricus.

In the east, a Roman ally in Palmyra, Odaenathus, succeeded in expelling the Persians from Roman territory but, after his death, his widow Zenobia took control of Syria in the name of her son, invaded Egypt, and extended Palmyrene rule from Asia Minor to the Nile. She proclaimed her son emperor in 271.

The hapless Gallienus, who ruled the Italy-centred residual empire alone after Valerian's capture, was murdered in 268. It was left to Aurelian (270–275) to restore the integrity of the Roman Empire by defeating Tetricus and Zenobia before he too was murdered.

A third-century 'fall of the Roman Empire' was averted, but the threat to Rome's frontiers had been raised by prolonged internal weakness and the succession issue remained unresolved. Four short-lived reigns later, the equestrian Diocletian (284–305) was proclaimed emperor by the army. He restored the empire's military strength and stability. In doing so, however, he irreparably weakened Rome's position as the imperial capital.

Diocletian transformed the empire into a military autocracy, increasing taxation to support a stronger army and an expanded imperial administration. He addressed the problems of emperors having to fight enemies on two fronts by selecting another army officer, Maximian, as his colleague, elevating him to the rank of fellow *Augustus* in 286. Diocletian focused on the eastern half of the empire and Maximian on the west, though the division remained informal.

They addressed the succession issue in 293 by the creation of two *Caesars*, subordinate rulers, Galerius supporting Diocletian and Constantius as the junior to Maximian. While Diocletian held the prime position in practice, the empire thus acquired four rulers (the tetrarchy, as it became known). They moved around the empire, according to military need, to keep their external enemies at bay. For this, they needed to be stationed in cities strategically much closer to the frontiers than Rome: Trier on the Rhine, Milan in north Italy, Sirmium close to the Danube, Nicomedia across the Bosphorus in Asia Minor, and Antioch in Syria. While Rome remained the official capital, Diocletian rarely visited it. In terms of imperial power politics, it had become irrelevant.[2]

The tetrarchy stabilised the empire and provided the foundation on which the fourth-century empire became stronger and more resilient. The succession issue was not altogether resolved, however. Diocletian and Maximian abdicated in favour of the two Caesars in 305, Diocletian rather more willingly than his colleague, but after the death of Constantius, a power struggle between contending claimants precipitated a further period of civil war. The ultimate victor was Constantine, whose reign began in 306—though it took him until 324 to defeat the last of his rivals.

Constantinople

Constantine entered Rome in triumph in 312, after his famous victory over the usurper Maxentius at Milvian Bridge, where his soldiers displayed the Christian monogram Chi-Rho on their shields. However, he soon left the city again and did not visit it again for fourteen years. The empire continued to be ruled from the tetrarchy's bases nearer the frontier. Galerius, a tetrarch who survived in power until his death in 311, for example, had his capital at Thessalonica.

Constantine's own power base had been in the west but, after he gained sole control of the empire in 324, he chose a new capital for himself in the east. He built up a 'New Rome' from the base of the small city of Byzantium on the strategically sited peninsula between the Bosphorus and the Sea of Marmara where Europe and Asia Minor converge.

Initially, Constantine probably intended this to be an imperial seat like Nicomedia or Sirmium had been for Diocletian, albeit rather more grandiose, rather than a direct rival to Rome. He invested major public resources in Rome, endowing it with Christian churches, and gave the city a Christian governor. However, his second visit there in 326, to celebrate twenty years of his reign, was not a success. The Romans resented the fact that that he had already celebrated the event in Nicaea in conjunction with the Ecumenical Council of the Christian Church there, and they were appalled by the oriental style of his court. Constantine deplored the continuing paganism of the Romans and refused to join their traditional procession to the Temple of Jupiter. It was probably after this that he decided to transform Byzantium into his new capital of Constantinople.

Constantinople had many advantages. The empire's economic centre of gravity was in the East; so was its most powerful enemy, Sassanid Persia. The barbarian threat from across the Danube could be countered more effectively from here than from Rome. The city's natural defences were promising. The peninsula was protected by water on two fronts and the land approach from the west could be sealed off by fortified city walls. The Golden Horn provided a well-shielded harbour. Water supply was a challenge but Roman aqueduct-building skills could rise to it. Politically and socially, a massive new development around a small pre-existing city made possible a capital that could be much more clearly Christian from the start.

The area marked out by Constantine's walls was five times the size of the former Byzantium. Constantine consciously modelled the new city on Rome so it had an

Column of Constantine, Constantinople (Istanbul), known as the Burnt Pillar, after a fire in the eighteenth century burned an already badly damaged monument. (*Bollweevil, own work, CC BY-SA 3.0*)

imperial palace, a new oval forum, a vast complex of government administrative buildings, a new Senate House, and a processional way with triumphal arches and statues. In the middle of the forum stood a column topped by a statue of Constantine as Apollo the sun-god.

Constantinople, however, was to be essentially Christian. Constantine began the construction of two great churches: St Sophia (the forerunner of Justinian's later church) and St Eirene (the Church of the Holy Apostles came later). The gladiatorial spectacles of Rome's Colosseum were eschewed as pagan but a huge Hippodrome capable of seating 80,000 spectators, with a loggia for the imperial family, was constructed for chariot-racing.

Constantinople was rapidly built up in advance of a formal dedication ceremony in 330. Art works were plundered from other Roman and Greek cities. The Serpent Column from Delphi was appropriated to adorn the Hippodrome. Religious relics included Noah's axe, Mary Magdalen's ointment, and fragments of the True Cross. Streets were laid out in a grid formation and housing constructed for, among others, senators who moved to the new seat of power, and under Constantine's successors, the city expanded rapidly.[3]

Ravenna's Decline

Meanwhile, what of Ravenna? During the first and second centuries, it had expanded markedly as a commercial port trading in ceramics, timber, olive oil, and wine, as well as serving as the Adriatic base for the Roman fleet whose provisioning was another major economic activity. During Trajan's reign, a 70-km aqueduct had been built. Canals were constructed to siphon water from the surrounding marshland and control flooding. While the ancient city walls had fallen into disrepair, Ravenna in the second century would have enjoyed peace. Like other Roman cities, it had a forum and other public buildings and temples: marble was brought in by sea for the production of monuments and sarcophagi.

However, also like other Roman cities, Ravenna suffered during the third-century crisis. Economic hardship, the debased coinage, and barbarian attacks disrupted its commerce. The Marcomanni attacked the city in 254 and another barbarian tribe invaded in 260. The plague also took a heavy toll. The city's population fell. Naval forces were of less importance in the warfare of the third century and the size of the fleet was reduced. By the early fourth century, Ravenna had lost some of its earlier distinction.

Before retiring to his splendid new palace across the Adriatic in Split, Diocletian visited Ravenna in 304, but he could scarcely have imagined that it would become the capital of the Western Empire within a hundred years.[4]

Divide and Rule?

Constantine discarded the idea of having joint Eastern and Western rulers. Once he had consolidated his power, he was the sole emperor, the *Augustus*, though his sons held junior positions as Caesars. Had his successors retained this degree of concentrated power, Rome might simply have been displaced by Constantinople as the imperial capital. For separate capitals to emerge to serve the Eastern and Western halves of the empire, imperial power had first to be divided. This now developed in response to continuing external threats on the Eastern and Western frontiers. The precedent was there in the tetrarchy and it was Constantine himself who helped it re-emerge.

Constantine had four sons: Crispus, by his first wife who died early, and three others (Constantine, Constantius, and Constans) by his second wife, Fausta. In 326, he killed first Crispus and then Fausta for reasons that remain unclear. Perhaps Crispus had a sexual relationship with his step-mother; perhaps she just alleged this in order to have him killed so that her own sons could succeed. Constantine decided nonetheless to recreate a tetrarchy of successors, consisting of Fausta's three sons and a nephew, Dalmatius. When he died in 337, each had been granted a group of provinces to govern. The three sons reallocated them among themselves after killing Dalmatius, but the arrangement was unstable. A period of civil war followed, involving a usurper called Magnentius, from which Constantius II emerged as the survivor.

As long as barbarians threatened to overrun the Rhine-Danube frontier, and the Sassanid Persian monarchy remained an active enemy in the east, it was impossible for a single emperor to rule without, at the very least, having a junior colleague with whom the military challenges could be shared. In 355, Constantius II appointed a young relative, Julian, as *Caesar* and sent him to war against the Alamanni in Gaul. Julian was very successful. His troops proclaimed him emperor, precipitating a civil war that ended with Constantius's death from natural causes. Julian (the Apostate) then became emperor (361–363) but was himself killed in warfare against the Persians. His successor extricated the Roman army only by negotiating a humiliating peace.

In 364, with continuing military threats on both the Eastern and Western fronts, the next emperor, Valentinian, revived the practice of joint emperors. He himself ruled in the west and he chose his brother Valens to be co-emperor in the east. Their strategy was to conclude treaties with the barbarians, alliances lubricated by subsidy. Valentinian concluded an agreement with the Alamanni in 374, while Valens had made a similar arrangement with the Goths on the Danube in 369. This left Valens free to campaign against Persia in the east.

In 376, this strategy fell apart. A great throng of Gothic warriors and refugees appeared on the bank of the Danube in two tribal bands: the Tervingi and the Greuthungi. Propelled by pressures from the Huns behind them and attracted by the safety and prosperity of the Roman Empire, they sought asylum. The Goths' request for asylum was relayed to Emperor Valens in Antioch. He knew that the Romans did not have enough troops available to handle the admission of so many migrants in a controlled fashion, so he ordered that terms be agreed for the Tervingi, who had volunteered to become Christians, but refused for the Greuthungi. However, when the Tervingi crossed the Danube into the empire, the Greuthungi followed.

The Romans then badly mismanaged the situation, precipitating unrest that turned to open conflict. Valens was compelled to make peace with the Persians so that he could return to Constantinople and marshal an army to lead against the Goths. By 378, he was ready. His brother Valentinian had died earlier and been succeeded by his young son Gratian and his infant half-brother Valentinian II. Valens requested Gratian to march to his assistance on the Danube with a second expeditionary force. Gratian agreed but then delayed to deal with a barbarian problem of his own on the Rhine. Meanwhile, the Goths had been joined by a force of Huns and Alans attracted by the prospect of plundering the empire's Balkan provinces. Valens decided to attack without waiting for Gratian. In the Battle of Adrianople in 378, he was disastrously defeated. The Roman army was massacred; Valens himself was killed and his body never found. The Goths rampaged inside the Roman Empire.[5]

Killing the emperor, however, did not give the Goths the settled home they sought. They marched on Constantinople but turned back after assessing its stout defences. Fighting continued but both the Goths and the Romans looked in the end for a negotiated solution. In 379, Gratian acquired a new co-emperor in the east, the army commander (Master of the Soldiers), Theodosius, and it was he who settled the Goths on a semi-autonomous basis in the Balkans, within the Roman Empire, giving them a privileged form of asylum in a negotiated peace treaty under which they could be required to serve in the Roman army.

Theodosius began his reign in 379 as effectively the Eastern emperor, the *de facto* successor to Valens. Gratian ruled in the west, nominally together with his young half-brother Valentinian II who succeeded him. Yet Theodosius expended his military energy—and the lives of his troops—primarily on defeating the armies of usurpers in the west, culminating in a major victory in the Battle of the Frigidus in 394 in which his Gothic troops bore the brunt of the fighting and suffered very heavy casualties.

Theodosius was the last in a series of military emperors to lead their Roman armies in person and he was to acquire the sobriquet of 'the Great'. He became sole ruler of the whole Roman Empire, but he concluded that the empire could only be effectively defended if it was divided into east and west. He had two sons whom he had named as his co-rulers in the east and west respectively and, when he died in 395, they duly jointly succeeded him. Both were boys. The new Eastern emperor, Arcadius, was eighteen and his brother, Honorius, the Western ruler, only ten. It is from their joint accession that the formal division of the Roman Empire into East and West dates.

The line of division between the provinces hardened. Separate administrations crystallised, separate armies were maintained, separate taxes were levied, and separate policies were adopted towards the different barbarian tribes. A divided empire required two capitals. Arcadius ruled the Eastern Empire from Constantinople. Rome remained a symbolic capital of the west but its imperial power had been lost: Honorius initially ruled the Western Empire from Milan. Ravenna at this point was just a modest city in Italy. What changed its fortune was a new incursion by the Goths.

Map of the Western and Eastern Roman Empires, AD 400.

The Choice of Ravenna

During Theodosius's later years, the Goths had become restless. Under a new leader, Alaric, they nurtured resentment over the scale of their losses at the Battle of the Frigidus and sought to renegotiate the terms of their settlement in compensation. Alaric demanded an appointment by the empire as a full Roman general, together with a guaranteed supply of food to his troops. When no Roman response to these demands was forthcoming, the Goths rebelled and from 395 to 397 they raided and pillaged in the Balkans. They tried to negotiate a new treaty with Eastern Emperor Arcadius in Constantinople, but Arcadius was a cipher in the hands of his courtiers. His Chamberlain, the eunuch Eutropius, initially conceded Alaric's demands, but a palace coup put an end to this appeasement.

Alaric in frustration then turned to the Western Empire where the regent for the young Emperor Honorius, and effective ruler, was the army commander Stilicho. His father had been a Vandal, but Stilicho had been brought up as a Roman and become a trusted general under Theodosius. He had married Theodosius's niece. He too rebuffed Alaric's demands. Alaric escalated the conflict. Choosing a time when

Stilicho was fighting another set of invaders further north, he led his army of Goths into northern Italy in 401. They reached the walls of Milan and laid siege to the city in which Emperor Honorius and his court resided. Stilicho returned to the rescue and defeated the Goths in two battles. The Goths withdrew back into the Balkans, but they had given the Western Empire a scare.

Now that Roman emperors no longer personally led their armies from the front, military leadership had passed to the generals. With military leadership went political power. Stilicho had been appointed regent by Theodosius and, given half an opportunity, he might have extended his power to the eastern half of the empire too. He had strengthened his position in 398 by arranging his daughter's marriage to Honorius but he had no ambition to usurp the imperial title.

Stilicho's position was a harbinger of future palace relationships. In the late third and early fourth centuries, a change was taking place in the upper ranks of the Roman military. Second-generation barbarians began emerging as the most senior generals, holding the rank of Master of the Soldiers. Due to their birth, they were not eligible to become emperors. Although barbarian blood was now to be found within the imperial family (Arcadius's wife Eudoxia was of Frankish origin, for example), a barbarian emperor would have lacked legitimacy in Roman eyes. Able barbarian generals at the head of Roman armies who hankered after supreme power could best achieve it by dominating young and inexperienced emperors. In the Eastern Empire, after Eutropius's fall, power fell, for a period, into the hands of Gainas, a general of Gothic descent. In the west, Stilicho managed the pliable Honorius, who was still a youth. The key to preserving his own rule was to maintain Honorius nominally in position.

When Alaric's Goths threatened Milan in 401, therefore, Stilicho's priority was to protect Honorius. It was this experience that prompted Stilicho and Honorius to relocate the imperial capital to Ravenna. The aim was not to station the emperor somewhere where he could engage the invading barbarians; it was to station him somewhere where the barbarians could not capture him.

So, in 402, Ravenna was chosen as an imperial capital where the Western emperor could be shielded. Surrounded by marshland, it was a much more defensible site than Milan. Through its port at Classe, it could be supplied by ship in the event of a siege since the barbarians were unable to challenge the Romans' command of the sea. In a dire emergency, the sea could also offer a means of escape.

Rome remained the symbolic capital and some members of the imperial family did choose to reside there. Some traditional government institutions still survived. The Senate continued to meet in Rome and Stilicho was later to need the help of wealthy senators in raising money quickly. The emperors continued to name Consuls annually, but their role was honorary and they could reside anywhere. While Rome's importance started to re-grow as the Popes developed their religious authority, however, it ceased to be the seat of Western imperial power. The Roman Empire had been a military autocracy for over a century and autocratic power was exercised from the city where the emperor resided, even if it was exercised by a military commander on the emperor's behalf. In the Western Empire, that city was now Ravenna.

Milan would have remained the Western capital had the requirement still been for a base from which the emperor could lead his troops into battle, but because emperors no longer did so, Ravenna was selected as the best place to keep a civilian emperor safe during the growing threat of barbarian incursions.

Ravenna in 402

The citizens of Ravenna must have been greatly surprised to have been given this honour. During the fourth century, the military importance of the fleet had continued to decline. The western end of the lagoon between Ravenna and Classe was beginning to silt up. Trade continued and the connection to Constantinople grew in significance, so Classe experienced some growth but Ravenna's prosperity had declined. Its high point, judging from the quality of the urban houses that have been excavated, had been during the second century. By the fourth century, the houses being built were smaller and the centre of economic activity shifted away from the old core of the city. Christianity had been established (we know of a Bishop Severus of Ravenna at work in the 340s), but there is no surviving evidence of any fourth century church-building.

Ravenna's character in 402, as best we can tell, was that of a somewhat run-down port. Essentially, Stilicho and Honorius selected as their new capital a coastal trading city that had seen better days. At the end of the fourth century, no citizen of Ravenna could have pictured the new city walls, palaces, cathedrals, churches, baptisteries, and mausoleums—with their glorious decoration—which were to arise.[6]

Imperial Ravenna and the Fall

The fall of the Western Roman Empire is conventionally dated AD 476, when its last emperor, Romulus Augustulus, was deposed. However, this is a symbolic date: by 476, most of the damage had been done. The main collapse took place during the earlier long reigns of two emperors: Honorius (395–423) and Valentinian III (425–455). Outer provinces were lost and Italy was subject to invasion by the Goths, the Huns, and the Vandals. A key figure astride the first half of the fifth century from Ravenna's perspective was Galla Placidia, Honorius's sister and Valentinian III's mother. She played a central political role in ensuring the succession of Valentinian III, a young boy at the time, for whom she then acted as regent. She was also the main imperial patron of church-building in Ravenna in her time. Before that, however, she had a dramatic early adult life as a hostage of the Goths.

After 402, Ravenna soon grew into its new imperial role and expanded. Honorius constructed a palace and the public buildings needed to support the imperial administration. Around 1,500 government officials are believed to have worked in Ravenna and new residences were constructed to house them. A circus was probably built as well. A mint was established for gold and silver coins, with another added later for bronze. The bishops of Ravenna built a grand cathedral, an associated baptistery and an episcopal palace—probably all the work of Bishop Ursus. New city walls were erected to enhance the city's defences.[1] Classe's importance as a port grew again. As intended, Ravenna became a haven in which the emperor could remain safe. Galla Placidia, however, initially lived in Rome.

Alaric the Goth

The empire was now hit by a series of military crises. Alaric the Goth, temporarily defeated by Stilicho after his attack on Milan, continued to rampage in the Balkans, still frustrated in his desire to be given the rank of a Roman general and to have the Roman state pay for feeding his troops. Stilicho had defeated him but had never fully vanquished his forces and Alaric remained a danger. In 405, Stilicho decided to grant him his military rank to keep him quiet while he tackled a new Gothic threat. In 405–6, a pagan Gothic king called Radagaisus, unconnected with Alaric, invaded Italy from the north with his own large force. He penetrated as far as Florence before Stilicho could defeat and kill him.

Shortly afterwards, in the winter of 406 came news that an alliance of Vandals, Suevi, and Alans had broken through the Rhine frontier, reportedly crossing the frozen river, and spread out into Gaul. This was not an isolated raid but an armed migration. One estimate is of an army of 20,000 or more warriors and a population of close to 100,000. They were probably pushed west by the move of the Huns from Asia into the Great Hungarian Plain. They were later joined by a large force of Burgundians. None of these tribes was ever expelled: the dismemberment of the Western Empire was beginning.

That same winter in Britain, the Roman army proclaimed a series of usurpers. The first two were swiftly killed but the third, called Constantine III, established a power base not only in Britain but across the Channel in Boulogne too. When the Vandals, Suevi, and Alans invaded Gaul, the Roman troops there switched their allegiance to him and they were then able to challenge the barbarian invaders. The effect was to drive the Vandals, Suevi, and Alans into southern Gaul and Spain, leaving Constantine III entrenched in western Gaul. Britain was now effectively lost to the empire.

In 408, Alaric decided to exploit Stilicho's multiplying crises by threatening to invade Italy again unless he was given 4,000 Roman pounds of gold. Stilicho agreed but it was a large sum to find swiftly. He plundered temples and other buildings in Rome and had to ask the wealthy Roman senators to help raise the money. The Senate agreed but under protest: one senator described it as a pact of slavery (*non est ista pax sed pactio servitutis*). Back in Ravenna, courtiers too bridled at giving in to Alaric's blackmail.

Also in 408, Eastern Emperor Arcadius died and his heir was his seven-year old son, Theodosius II. Stilicho, who had long been thought to have ambitions to take power in the east, decided to go to Constantinople in the hope of becoming regent there too. He asked Honorius, who was now twenty-three, to commission Alaric to fight the usurper Constantine III. The Ravenna court and the army, already indignant at Stilicho's gold payment to Alaric, were outraged at his priorities. Confronting Constantine III, who was ensconced in power in Britain, much of Gaul and part of Spain, was Stilicho's responsibility. His motive in evading it was highly suspect: a palace politician called Olympius accused him of plotting to take over the Eastern Empire. Olympius persuaded Honorius to order Stilicho's arrest. Stilicho sought refuge in a Ravenna church, but to no avail; he was executed. Soon afterwards, his son, who had been betrothed to Honorius's sister, Galla Placidia, was also killed.

The Sack of Rome

Olympius repudiated Stilicho's policy of appeasing Alaric and so Alaric, with his brother-in-law Athaulf, led his Goth army back into Italy and laid siege to Rome, cutting off its main food supplies. He demanded, and was paid, a further ransom of gold and silver. Alaric's main desire, however, was to open negotiations with Honorius. Meeting an imperial plenipotentiary in Rimini, he demanded a senior imperial generalship, regular food supplies, and the right to settle his Gothic followers in Roman provinces to the north-east of Italy.

When Honorius balked, Alaric renewed his siege of Rome and raised the stakes. He connived with the Senate to elect a new emperor, Attalus. Attalus appointed Alaric to be the empire's chief general and Alaric laid siege to Ravenna, aiming to depose Honorius. However, 4,000 Eastern Empire troops came to Ravenna's rescue. Alaric then returned to Rome to besiege it for the third time. He deposed Attalus, who had been unable to give him what he wanted, and this time, in 410, he led his army into Rome to plunder the city. He was admitted through the Salerian Gate. The citizens of Rome, having been blockaded and starved during Alaric's two previous sieges, had no appetite for further resistance. Many fled as refugees and the city's population dropped dramatically.[2]

For three days, Alaric's warriors rampaged through Rome's streets, seizing goods and burning buildings, though, as the Goths were Arian Christians, Alaric ordered strict respect for churches and for the clergy. The damage Alaric inflicted on the empire's prestige was greater than the harm caused by his marauding troops. The sack of Rome shocked the world: the symbolic capital of the Roman Empire had not been invaded since a force of marauding Gauls had attacked it eight centuries earlier in 390 BC. Writing from the Holy Land, St Jerome bewailed the decapitation of the Roman Empire 'when the bright light of all the world was put out' and 'the whole world perished in one city'.[3]

This was the point at which the Church clearly uncoupled itself from the empire. Pagan Romans had blamed Christianity, and its banishment of the traditional gods who had guarded the city, for the disaster. It was to combat this charge that St Augustine composed his *City of God*, pointing out all the previous crises from which the pagan gods had provided no protection. He also advised Christians not to regard Rome as eternal. The heavenly city, in which Christians should place their faith, was not the earthly city of Rome:

> Christ with divine authority denounces and condemns the offences of men, and their perverted lusts, and he gradually withdraws his family from all parts of a world which is failing and declining through those evils, so he may establish a city whose titles of 'eternal' and 'glorious' are not given by meaningless flattery but by the judgment of truth.[4]

The community of Christians was not synonymous with the Roman Empire. The Church of the faithful was not tied to the imperial secular regime.

After three days, Alaric withdrew his army, still not having achieved his objectives, and marched his army south, perhaps intending to cross via Sicily to the empire's breadbasket province of Africa. He took with him a highly valuable hostage: Galla Placidia, then in her early twenties.

Sheltered in Ravenna, Honorius was powerless to prevent either the sack of Rome or the capture of his sister. The empire at this juncture did not have the military strength to overcome the Goths. A sizeable group of barbarian troops in the Roman army had deserted to join Alaric, as had a number of slaves. Honorius has had a bad press in history, judged as essentially ineffectual. He was apparently fond of tending chickens. Procopius, writing in the sixth century, records that he had a chicken called Rome and, when informed that disaster had befallen the city of Rome, had at first feared that his fowl 'Rome' had perished.[5]

Galla Placidia: Captive

As an imperial family member, Galla Placidia would have been treated well. Alaric intended to use her to put more and more pressure on Honorius until he secured his demands, but then, unexpectedly, he died.

After Alaric's death, the Gothic leadership passed to his brother-in-law Athaulf, who led his followers out of Italy and into Gaul, taking Galla Placidia with him. Although the Vandals and their allies were now moving into Spain, Gaul was still a battlefield in which the usurper Constantine III was at large. Honorius sent a Roman army led by Flavius Constantius, a former follower of Stilicho, against Constantine. The usurper was captured, sent in chains to Ravenna and beheaded *en route*. Then another usurper arose, initially with the support of Athaulf's Goths. Constantius persuaded Athaulf to change sides, the usurper was captured and beheaded, and the Goths again began negotiations with the Romans.

Athaulf was to be granted the right to settle his people in Aquitania in southern Gaul. However, when the Romans were unable to supply the corn that the Goth insisted on as part of the agreement, Athaulf broke off talks.

Like his predecessor Alaric, Athaulf really wanted acceptance as a leading figure within the Roman Empire. He reportedly said that he had once wanted to blot out the name of Rome and replace its territory with the new empire of Gothia, but that he had now changed his mind. He despaired of the Goths' 'unbridled barbarism' and their inability to obey state laws. He had therefore decided to restore the Roman Empire to its full strength by infusing it with Gothic vigour. He revived support for Alaric's former puppet Emperor Attalus, but, much more significantly, he married Galla Placidia, reportedly with her consent.

In 414, Athaulf and Galla Placidia were wedded in Narbonne in a ceremony in which not only was Galla Placidia dressed in the Roman manner but so was Athaulf, who wore a Roman general's cloak. In due course, Galla Placidia gave birth to their son who was christened Theodosius. He was the grandson of Theodosius the Great and the nephew of Honorius, who was childless. Did Athaulf and Galla Placidia see their newborn son as Honorius's heir?

The Romans could not ignore this provocation, so Constantius blockaded the Goths and deprived them of food supplies, causing the Goths to move into Spain. Then, in quick succession, the baby Theodosius died, Athaulf was murdered, his successor repudiated Galla Placidia, this successor was murdered in turn, and the next Goth leader, Wallia, reopened negotiations with the empire.[6]

In 415, a deal was done. Constantius supplied the Goths with corn. Wallia agreed to return Galla Placidia, now a childless widow, to the Romans. The Goths would also help fight other barbarian invaders in Spain and they were subsequently rewarded formally with their territory in Aquitania (becoming known to us as the Visigoths). On the face of it, Constantius had achieved a remarkable restoration of the empire's fortunes after the low point of 410, but the regime had been seriously weakened both by loss of territory and by the economic damage inflicted by warfare. In 412, Honorius had to reduce by four-fifths the level of taxation in the five provinces of Italy which had been hardest hit. Reduced tax revenue in turn weakened the army, by now largely composed of barbarians.

Galla Placidia: Empress

In 417, Galla Placidia somewhat reluctantly, and at her brother's insistence, married Constantius. A year later, she gave birth to their daughter, Honoria, and, the following year, to a son, Valentinian.

In 421, Honorius promoted Constantius to the rank of *Augustus*, becoming his co-emperor, and Galla Placidia was named as empress (*Augusta*). However, later that same year, Constantius died. Amid the in-fighting to find a military leader who could succeed him, Galla Placidia tried to stay close to her brother but she was targeted by court enemies and, when her entourage of Goths clashed with some Roman soldiers during street riots in Ravenna, she and Honorius quarrelled. In 422, she was banished with her son, seeking refuge at the court of Eastern Emperor Theodosius II in Constantinople. She was there in 425 when Honorius died.

This whole saga illustrates how complex the relationship between the Romans and the Goths had become. To see the Goths simply as blackmailing foreign invaders who sacked Rome is to miss a significant part of the picture: Goths were not only inside the Roman Empire where they were opportunistically used as military allies, but many were inside the Roman army and a few were inside the imperial court.

The death of Honorius leaving as heir the six-year old Valentinian, in exile with his mother in Constantinople, almost inevitably produced a usurper, this time called John. Theodosius II refused to recognise him and sent an expeditionary army to Italy to oust him and install the boy as Emperor Valentinian III, with Galla Placidia as regent and empress. John was executed and Valentinian was betrothed to Theodosius's daughter. The role of Constantinople in the determining the regime in Ravenna was a harbinger of future east–west relationships.

John had commissioned a Roman general named Aetius, who had grown up as a hostage among the Huns, to recruit a Hunnic force to support him. By the time Aetius and his Huns arrived in Ravenna, however, John had been defeated. Galla Placidia bribed the Huns to depart and gave Aetius a military post.

In the past, most power struggles had been for the position of emperor. In the fifth century, however, when the emperors no longer led from the front, a key contest was for the position of supreme military commander. Under Galla Placidia and her young son, there was now a vacancy. Eventually, Aetius emerged in this role but only after a period of rivalry during which the empire's external defences were weakened.

Critically, the Vandals, in alliance with the Alans, crossed from Spain into North Africa, leaving the Suevi in Spain, and the Franks and the Alamanni in Gaul, along with the Visigoths who had rebelled again. The Burgundians invaded Belgica.

Due to its economic importance as a source of grain, the loss of Africa was particularly serious. An army from the Eastern Empire landed in Carthage and challenged the Vandal leader Geiseric, forcing him to conclude an armistice limiting the Vandal and Alan territory in Africa. This left Aetius free to regain a measure of imperial control in the north-west provinces. He again made use of his Hunnic connections. The Huns were granted some territory in the Balkans and then used as allies against the Visigoths, the Franks, the Alamanni and the Burgundians. The Rhine frontier was strengthened, and an accommodation reached with the Suevi in Spain.

It was another imperial military recovery but then in 439 came a hammer blow—a further Vandal attack in North Africa, leading to the fall of Carthage. A joint Eastern-Western Empire fleet and army was assembled in Sicily for a major expedition against the Vandals, but, because of a threat from the Huns, the Eastern Empire withdrew its forces and it never sailed. Instead, a new treaty was made with Geiseric. Not only was he recognised as a 'client king' of the empire, but his eldest son was betrothed to Valentinian III's daughter, Eudocia, another example of the ambivalence and complexity of Roman-barbarian relationships.

With Valentinian III an adult and Aetius ensconced in power, Galla Placidia ceased to play a major political role but she continued actively to support the Church.

Galla Placidia: Church Patron

While Honorius had constructed the secular public buildings in Ravenna, Galla Placidia was the imperial patron supporting the building of churches, working closely with Bishop Peter I (known as '*Chrysologus*', meaning 'golden word'). She had already contributed to the renovation of two churches in Rome and, in Ravenna, she built the church of Santa Croce, probably around 420 before her quarrel with Honorius and flight to Constantinople.

Soon after 425, she founded San Giovanni Evangelista and had it decorated with mosaics (now destroyed) that told the story of her and her children's escape from the danger of shipwreck in a storm by appealing to St John the Evangelist. An inscription recounted that she, Valentinian, and Honoria constructed the church in fulfilment of a vow.[7] The date of their near-disaster is unclear: it may have been during their voyage back from Constantinople after Honorius's death. Valentinian III owed his throne to the support he and Galla Placidia were given by Eastern Emperor Theodosius II. Portraits of Theodosius II and his predecessor Arcadius and of their wives featured in the apse of San Giovanni Evangelista. This portrayal of members of the imperial family in churches indicated the strength of the Eastern Empire's influence in Ravenna.

Although the Church in the west had begun to uncouple itself from the empire, in Constantinople the emperor continued to be seen as God's ruler on earth.

What Galla Placidia is best known for, of course, is the construction of the Mausoleum linked to her name, now one of Ravenna's eight UNESCO heritage sites. It is uncertain whether it was designed as a mortuary chapel or as an oratory. It is also uncertain how direct an association it had with Galla Placidia. It is possible that it was built with the intention of housing her tomb—and, in later centuries, a muddled legend grew that she was buried here—but in 450, she died in Rome and is believed to have been buried there. What is now known is that the mausoleum or chapel was originally linked to the church of Santa Croce, which Galla Placidia did build and where she is known to have regularly prayed.

Externally, the mausoleum is elegant, small, and simple, constructed in brick in the shape of a cross. Internally, it is dimly lit but gloriously decorated in mosaic, by artists from Rome, Milan, or possibly Constantinople. The barrel-vaulted ceilings of the arms of the cross are decorated ornamentally with flowers against a dark indigo background. On the wall over the entrance, a young beardless Christ is portrayed as the Good Shepherd in a rocky setting surrounded by sheep.

On the opposite wall facing the entrance is a figure long believed to be St Lawrence, beside the flaming griddle on which he was martyred, though this interpretation has

Mausoleum of Galla Placidia, with Santa Croce behind. (*Author's collection*)

Above: Mausoleum of Galla Placidia, Christ as the Good Shepherd. (*vvoe/Shutterstock.com*)

Below: Mausoleum of Galla Placidia, probably, but contestably, St Lawrence. (*ribeiroantonio/Shutterstock.com*)

Mausoleum of Galla Placidia, cupola. (*JIPEN/Shutterstock.com*)

been challenged inconclusively by modern scholars. One suggestion is that the figure could be Christ, another that it could be St Vincent of Saragossa.[8]

The central cupola has an indigo sky in which hang golden stars in circles decreasing in size towards the centre where a gold cross shines. Around the base of the cupola are the four creatures of the Apocalypse (the lion, the ox, the man, and the eagle), which had come to be associated with the four evangelists.

Although Galla Placidia herself is not here, the mausoleum does house three ancient Roman sarcophagi. Though of very different styles, they are believed to date from the fifth century. The visitor is told that they are the 'so-called' sarcophagi of Galla Placidia, either her brother Honorius or her son Valentinian III, and her husband Constantius, but there is no foundation for these attributions.[9]

Huns and Vandals

The 450s were a traumatic decade for Italy, and for Rome especially, to which Valentinian III had moved his residence in the 450, but, by virtue of its location, Ravenna remained safe on the side line.

The Huns were fierce and savage nomadic warriors, who fought mainly as mounted archers but had the skills and the weaponry to attack walled cities too. They had migrated from the steppes of Asia to the Black Sea and then Hungary and the Danube, terrorising and subjugating all the tribes in their path. Their impact on the Roman Empire had initially been to push the Goths and other tribes westward into the imperial territory. Now the Huns had rampaged along the Danube and advanced east as far as Constantinople. Eastern Emperor Theodosius II agreed to pay them 6,000 pounds of gold and a further 2,000 pounds annually to keep them at bay.

By raiding, plundering, and blackmailing their way across Eurasia the Huns created an empire of their own, with its centre in the Hungarian plain. It was essentially an agglomeration of mobile warriors, held together by the booty with which the leaders were able to reward their followers. The Hunnic joint kings were Attila and his brother Bleda, until Attila killed Bleda and ruled supreme.

Attila's thirst for war had no limits. He regarded the gold that Theodosius was giving him not as a bribe but as tribute to the victor. Notwithstanding the Huns' relationship with Aetius, he decided to attack the Western Empire, and he found a convenient pretext. Honoria, Galla Placidia's daughter, had become pregnant through an affair with her estate manager and had been married off, against her will, to an elderly senator. In 450, she appealed to Attila for help and sent him a brooch or a ring and a letter which Attila chose to interpret as a proposal of marriage.

Attila began by terrorising Gaul but, after losing to Aetius at the battle of Chalons in 451, he led his warriors into Italy, razing the city of Aquileia at the head of the Adriatic. The Huns then waged war across northern Italy, sacking Padua, Mantua, Vicenza, Verona, Brescia, Bergamo, and, after a long siege, Milan. Ravenna was left alone. Attila almost certainly contemplated an attack on Rome but his army could get no further than the river Po, halted as much by starvation in an Italian famine as by the Roman army. Then in 453, Attila unexpectedly died. With no clear successor, his empire, a war-making machine without roots, swiftly collapsed.

When the Hun threat receded, Valentinian III decided to end his subservient relationship to Aetius. Together with a co-conspirator, he stabbed him to death. Six months later, Valentinian III himself was murdered in revenge by Petronius Maximus, who was proclaimed his successor. In search of some pretence of legitimacy, Petronius Maximus arranged for his son to become engaged to Eudocia, Valentinian III's daughter. She, however, had already been betrothed by treaty to the son of the Vandal king, Geiseric.

Outraged, Geiseric led a Vandal fleet in an attack on Rome in 455. The Vandals sacked the city much more damagingly than Alaric had done. Petronius Maximus fled and was killed. Gold and other valuables were looted and loaded onto the Vandal ships. So too were several captives including the widow and daughters of Valentinian III, enabling Geiseric's son to marry Eudocia.[10]

During the two long reigns of Honorius and Valentinian III, power had rested with a trio of military commanders: Stilicho, Constantius (Galla Placidia's husband), and Aetius. Notwithstanding the abilities of these commanders, it was during this half-century that the Western Empire received military and economic wounds from which it would never recover. However, in Ravenna, which had been spared any sacking by the Huns or the Vandals, the Church continued to build. After Galla Placidia's death, imperial patronage of church-building had ceased but the Church in Ravenna, backed by wealthy donors, no longer needed imperial support. It was during the dying decades of the Western Roman Empire that another one of Ravenna's religious masterpieces was completed.

The Neonian Baptistery

This was the work of Bishop Neon (450–473) who renovated and redecorated the baptistery originally founded by Bishop Ursus, linked to the adjacent cathedral (known as the Ursiana). Baptism was an important ceremony during this period, when conversion to Christianity from paganism was still continuing: only the bishop could conduct the service. In reconstructing the Ravenna baptistery, Neon is thought to have been following the example of Pope Sixtus III who had redecorated the Lateran baptistery, and to have been emphasising the religious status of Ravenna during a period when the Popes were strengthening their prestige in Rome.

Built in brick, the baptistery has an octagonal structure and sits beside the tenth-century bell tower belonging to the cathedral. Inside, the ground floor is almost wholly taken up by a huge font, big enough to accommodate immersed adults.

High above, the decoration of the cupola in marble and mosaic is magnificent. Its central medallion portrays the baptism of Christ in the Jordan River. A small figure beside Christ and John the Baptist represents the Jordan River. Around this scene,

Neonian Baptistery font, only partly original. (*Author's collection*)

Neonian Baptistery, with bell-tower of cathedral behind. (*Comune of Ravenna*)

Neonian Baptistery, cupola. (*Dmytro Surkov/Shutterstock.com*)

twelve apostles process in two groups led by Peter and Paul and around them is an outer ring in which thrones and altars, separated by acanthus plants, alternate. The figures are lively and expressive. Amid the chaos elsewhere, Ravenna was clearly able to attract and sustain artists and craftsmen of the highest order.

End of the Imperial Line

The Western Empire was now tottering. Its last twenty years were ignominious. Emperors came and went. Another military general of barbarian origin, Ricimer, wielded the real power until his death in 472. Emperors were chosen and deposed on his say-so. After Petronius Maximus's flight, Avitus was proclaimed emperor with Visigothic support but Ricimer deposed him. Ricimer chose another soldier, his colleague Majorian, as emperor, and supported him when he restored order to Gaul but arrested and executed him when he lost his fleet in an unsuccessful attempt to invade Geiseric's Vandal kingdom in Africa. Ricimer's next candidate, Libius Severus, died and two years elapsed before he agreed with Eastern Emperor Leo I on the appointment of a successor, Anthemius, whose daughter Ricimer married.

However, after the disastrous failure of a joint east and west attack on Vandal Africa, Ricimer overthrew his father-in-law, replacing him in 472 with Olybrius. Later that year, both Ricimer and Olybrius died and Ricimer's barbarian nephew put Glycerius on the throne. Leo I contested this, however, and in 474 replaced Glycerius with Julius Nepos. By then, the Western Empire had shrunk to little more than Italy, a couple of provinces to its north and Pannonia and Dalmatia in the Balkans. Two major naval initiatives to defeat the Vandals in Africa had foundered. Spain had been lost to the Visigoths and the Suevi. Gaul had been lost, primarily to the Visigoths, the Burgundians, and the Franks. Britain had long been lost.

It was not just the Church that had begun to distance itself from the Western imperial regime: so too had the land-owning aristocracy. In the lost provinces, the wealthy Roman owners of large estates, no longer protected by the Roman state and its laws, had to come to terms with their Visigoth, Burgundian, or other barbarian rulers. In Italy, too, the well-to-do senatorial class retreated from the cities to their country villas and opted out of imperial politics. Commercial ties across the western Mediterranean were shrinking, agriculture had been disrupted by warfare, cities remained damaged by sieges, and the loss of Africa as a major supplier of grain to Italy had a severe impact. As the tax base continued to contract, lack of revenue hampered army recruitment and disrupted army pay.

By now, the Roman army consisted largely of barbarians, mainly drawn from Germanic tribes, such as the Sciri, who had moved into Italy after the collapse of the Hunnic empire and been recruited by Ricimer. In 474, the new emperor, Julius Nepos, appointed Orestes, a Roman who had served under Attila the Hun, to command them. Orestes cynically used his predominantly barbarian army to depose Julius Nepos, who fled to the Eastern Empire. In his place, Orestes elevated his own young son, Romulus. Thus Romulus Augustulus (as he became known) became the last Western Roman emperor in 475. Power, of course, lay in the hands of Orestes.

The Germanic troops, however, were not being paid regularly. They rebelled, electing one of their own officers, Odoacer, a Sciri by background, as their leader. They had noted how the Visigoths had been settled, with grants of land, in Gaul and were now prospering as peasant-soldiers. They demanded that Orestes make a settlement in Italy for their benefit, granting them land under the Roman concept of *hospitalitas*, which had been developed for immigrants whom the Romans wished to welcome, and which involved Roman 'hosts' donating land to the newcomers. When Orestes refused the soldiers' demands, Odoacer killed him. He then organised sufficient grants of land to satisfy his followers and, as the new *de facto* Roman military commander, he assumed Orestes's position of power.

Odoacer saw no need to keep Romulus Augustulus emperor and deposed him in 476. He told Eastern Emperor Zeno that the west did not need an emperor, sent him the imperial insignia of office, and asked to be put in charge of Italy himself. Zeno demurred, since he still backed Julius Nepos, but he was in no position to intervene and anyway Nepos died a few years later. The barbarian Odoacer became the self-appointed King of Italy and the Western Roman Empire fell.

Odoacer's rule was characterised by tolerance and continuity. He allowed Romulus Augustulus to live in peace in Campania. Whatever strategy he used to acquire land for his barbarian troops was accomplished without provoking the Roman landowning aristocracy into revolt. He preserved the existing regional and administrative framework. He issued coins initially with the head of Julius Nepos. He maintained the role of the Senate and appointed Romans to senior government offices. Though an Arian himself, Odoacer had no quarrel with the Pope or the orthodox Catholic Church. He also halted the contraction of the former Western Empire, recovering Sicily from the Vandals and extending his own rule in Dalmatia.

Ravenna's Capital Status

Before the fall, Ravenna's role as the imperial capital had become a sporadic one. After Galla Placidia's death in 450, Valentinian III had moved back to Rome. His successors, Petronius Maximus and Avitus, also chose to reside in Rome. Majorian and Libius Severus restored imperial rule from Ravenna but Anthemius and Olybrius returned to Rome. Glycerius then ruled from Ravenna, Julius Nepos from Rome, and Romulus Augustulus from Ravenna.[11]

However, after the fall, Ravenna became the regal capital of Italy. Odoacer moved into Ravenna's imperial palace and ruled from there. He was to reign without challenge for thirteen years. This was not a period when any great new buildings were constructed in Ravenna but, critically, it was a period when existing buildings were preserved. The capital had changed hands without civil war. More broadly, it was a period that demonstrated the possibility of a Romanised barbarian ruling Romans through Roman institutions.

AD 476, when Romulus Augustulus was deposed, is a landmark date by which historians mark the fall of the Western Empire but it was not a date at which life changed dramatically for most Romans. Under Odoacer's Romanised rule, daily life in Italy continued much as before. For Ravenna, however, 476 was the date at which its position as a capital city was firmly restored; indeed, it was after 476 that the city was to enjoy its greatest period of church-building and decoration.

Ostrogoth Ravenna

The idea of a barbarian ruling the Romans by maintaining Roman laws and institutions was brought to full fruition under the regime that succeeded Odoacer—the long reign of Theodoric the Ostrogoth (493–526). Theodoric's achievement was unique among the barbarian kingdoms that replaced the Western Roman Empire and lies at the heart of the explanation of Ravenna's ability to construct fine churches and glorious mosaic decoration during the conflict and upheaval surrounding the end of the Western Empire.

Theodoric sustained the three strands of continuity we identified in Chapter Two. He maintained Ravenna's position as a capital city and enriched it with his own secular and religious buildings. Theodoric built Arian churches but, importantly, he also established an ethos of religious tolerance that allowed the orthodox Catholic Church to continue its own separate church-building. In his own person, through his upbringing, he embodied both Gothic and Roman values and was able to create an exceptionally successful Romano-Gothic state. The initiative that brought him to Italy and Ravenna began with the Eastern emperor.

Zeno and the Ostrogoths

At the end of the fourth century, when the ailing Emperor Theodosius bequeathed the eastern half of the Roman Empire to his elder son Arcadius and the western to the younger Honorius, he reaffirmed the seniority of the East. Ravenna, as the Western imperial capital, could never rival Constantinople. After deposing Romulus Augustulus, Odoacer had respected this precedence in sending the imperial insignia to Constantinople and asking Eastern Emperor Zeno to legitimise his own rule over Italy.

However, Zeno withheld his endorsement of Odoacer even after Julius Nepos's death. He was confronting a rival of his own in Constantinople called Illus, whose rebellion in 484 led to civil war in Asia Minor and who may have sought Odoacer's support. Zeno, in need of allies of his own, courted a group of Goths within the Eastern Empire who became known as the Ostrogoths.

The Ostrogoths had been subjects of Attila the Hun and, in the aftermath of his death, had emerged in two distinct groups inside the empire in the Balkans. They played power games with Zeno and his rivals and with one another but around 482 came together under the leadership of Theodoric the Amal whose followers had been rampaging in the area around Thessalonica. Zeno sought an alliance with him and in 483 offered him generous terms. The Ostrogoths were granted lands where they could settle and Zeno made Theodoric a consul, an unusually high honour for a barbarian. Theodoric helped fight Zeno's rival, Illus, who was killed in 484, and Zeno then appointed him as an imperial general.[1]

It was, however, an alliance of convenience: Theodoric had further ambitions and Zeno did not trust him. Theodoric had grown up in Constantinople. He had been taken there as a hostage from the age of seven or eight, as part of a peace deal between the Goths and the Eastern Empire, and remained there for ten years, receiving a Roman education and learning a great deal about Roman government. Now, as leader of the united Ostrogoths, Theodoric sought greater land and wealth and a permanent position of power within the Eastern Empire. In 486, he defied Zeno by allowing his Ostrogoth followers to ravage Thrace. The following year, he advanced on Constantinople with his army, trying to pressure Zeno in much the same way that Alaric had tried to pressure Honorius in the west eighty years earlier.

The Ostrogoth Invasion of Italy

Zeno decided that he needed to act boldly to remove Theodoric as a threat. Instead of offering him a place of greater honour within the Eastern Empire, he proposed that Theoderic lead his followers out of the Balkans into Italy where he could overthrow Odoacer and rule there himself. Theodoric realised that Zeno would never willingly agree to grant him what he wanted and would try to overturn any arrangement made under duress, so the prospect of ruling in Italy appealed to him.

Theodoric set off for Italy with all his people (women and children, cattle and sheep) as well as his warriors. Odoacer's army lay in wait for him. Theodoric won the initial skirmishes in 489 and Odoacer retreated to the protection of Ravenna. Aided by a perfidious general, Odoacer was able to counterattack and Theodoric had to call on Visigoth help to avoid an early defeat. Theodoric then pushed Odoacer back into Ravenna and laid siege to the city, but for three years, he was unable to break through its well-established defences.

In 493, with the capital now facing famine, Bishop John of Ravenna brokered a negotiated settlement under which power was to be shared. He then opened the city gates to Theodoric. Ten days later, Theodoric invited Odoacer to a banquet and personally killed him with his sword. Odoacer's family were despatched: his wife to prison where she died, his brother killed, and his son captured and later executed. A massacre of Odoacer's closest supporters followed and thus Theodoric the Ostrogoth became the ruler of Italy on the Eastern emperor's behalf.

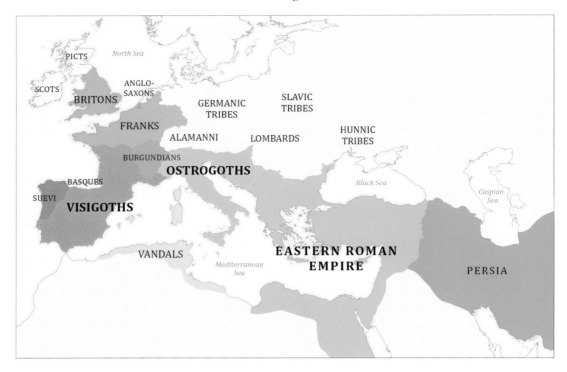

Map of the Roman Empire and Barbarian Europe, AD 500.

Basis of Theodoric's Rule

Zeno had died in 491 so Theodoric now sent ambassadors to his successor, Anastasius. After a delay that had less to do with regal legitimacy than with papal politics, Anastasius formally recognised Theodoric's position in 497 and returned the imperial insignia to Ravenna. Theodoric was recognised as king, not as emperor, owing allegiance to Constantinople; this would be important for the future.

Theodoric had gained his title by force and by perfidy. He had also used threats, warning Roman landowners that he would disinherit any of them who supported Odoacer. After his victory, however, he needed a more solid foundation for his regime. As a barbarian attempting to rule the Italian rump of the former Western Roman Empire he had to reconcile and satisfy three constituencies: his own barbarian followers, the Romans, and the Eastern emperor in Constantinople. Odoacer had managed to reconcile the first two but failed with the third.

Theodoric learned the lesson. He did not evict Odoacer's followers from their settlements but incorporated them into the Ostrogothic tribe. He then had to settle his own followers, numbering perhaps around 100,000. How this was achieved has been the subject of academic debate. The Roman concept of *hospitalitas*, under which Roman 'hosts' donated shares of their estates to newcomers, may have been followed as the basis for a settlement. This would, however, have risked provoking fury among the Roman landowners and been unsatisfactory both economically and socially. Alternatively, the Romans may have been taxed in order to fund grants with which the Goths could buy their own land.[2] Young male Goths were also paid to be available for military service. The Goths congregated in specific areas, mostly in northern and central Italy, where they developed their own agriculture and provided garrisons.

Ruling the 4 million or so Romans in Italy was the bigger challenge. He needed to win their loyalty. Theodoric ensured that they continued to live as Roman citizens under their own laws. He brought Roman senators, most famously Cassiodorus, into his administration. He behaved in effect as the successor to the Western emperors, shedding his barbarian garb and clothing himself in the imperial purple. He constructed a grand new palace in Ravenna and two other palaces in Pavia and Verona.

In 500, he visited Rome and was welcomed by the Pope and the Senate whom he treated with great courtesy. He promised publicly to uphold the achievements of previous Roman emperors. He laid on circus games, distributed grain to the people and provided funding for the restoration of public buildings. Notwithstanding his Arian beliefs, he forged good relationships with the orthodox Catholic Church and fostered the imperial ideology of the sacred Christian ruler: like the Eastern Roman emperor, he wanted to be revered.

In deference to Constantinople, however, he refrained from issuing imperial laws himself, promulgating edicts instead. He minted gold coins featuring the head of the Eastern emperor and shared with the Eastern emperor the role of nominating consuls. Flattery was not neglected. Cassiodorus recorded for posterity a letter he drafted for Theodoric to send to Emperor Anastasius in 508:

> You are the fairest ornament of all realms, you are the healthful defence of the whole world, to which all other rulers rightfully look up with reverence. We above all, who by Divine help learned in Your Republic the art of governing Romans with equity … Our royalty is an imitation of yours, modelled on your good purpose, a copy of the only Empire …[3]

Theodoric knew that a respectful relationship with the Eastern Empire was one of the keys to maintaining power in his own quasi-empire.

One State, Two Nations

The regime Theodoric constructed was a single state of two largely separate peoples, divided by language, religion (Arian and orthodox Catholic), laws, customs, and culture. He was in effect both King of Italy and King of the Ostrogoths. For military purposes, Theodoric relied primarily on the Goths, while his administrative civil service was staffed largely by Romans. Theodoric could not grant Roman citizenship to a Goth or appoint a Goth to the Senate.

It is difficult to imagine that the Romans did not deeply resent their Gothic conquerors and no doubt they considered themselves culturally far superior. Unless they were serving in the imperial administration, the Roman aristocracy stayed in Rome or on their country estates, rather than in Theodoric's Ravenna. However, neither the orthodox Catholic Church nor the landed aristocracy had been wedded to the western imperial administration and the Romans were well accustomed to barbarians as military leaders, so they tacitly accepted Ostrogoth rule. With the Church taking on an expanded public welfare role, the impact on day-to-day Roman life was limited.

For the most part, the two communities remained separate, each under its own laws, but new procedures needed to be developed for dealing with legal disputes between Goths and Romans. There was some intermarriage, educated Goths learned Latin, though few Romans learned Gothic. As Theodoric observed, 'An able Goth wants to be like a Roman; only a poor Roman would want to be like a Goth'.[4]

Ostrogoth Italy generally prospered. Ravenna, as its capital, expanded, reaching its maximum ancient population of around 10,000, with Goths living alongside Roman civil servants and other professionals linked to the court.[5] Theodoric invested in public works, draining marshland, repairing Ravenna's aqueduct, improving the port at Classe, and constructing new public buildings. Nor was investment in Rome neglected. The regime's two-nation structure was to prove fragile, but Theodoric managed to make it work. Procopius, writing later during Justinian's reign, praises Theodoric's regard for law, justice, and security, extols his 'wisdom and manliness' and records that 'love for him among both Goths and Italians grew to be great'.[6]

The Former Western Empire

Theodoric consolidated his kingdom's hold on Sicily and enlarged its territory in Dalmatia, but he had a wider perspective too. He constructed a network of alliances with the other barbarian kings who now ruled fragments of the old Western Empire. He did this through family marriages.

His link to the Franks was through his own marriage to Audefleda, sister of Clovis, their king. His relationship with the Visigoths rested on the marriage of his daughter, Theodegotha, to the Visigoth King Alaric II. His tie to the Burgundians was through the marriage of another daughter, Ostrogotho Areagni, to the Burgundian king's son, Sigismund. Then he brought the Vandals into the network by having his widowed sister, Amalafrida, marry the widower Vandal King Thrasamund.[7]

These relationships were not strong enough to hold all the ex-imperial regimes together: in 507, Clovis attacked the Visigoths and seized Aquitaine, pushing the Visigoths down into Spain. However, in the aftermath of this, Theodoric brought the Visigothic kingdom in effect under his own rule. Ostrogoth garrisons were established

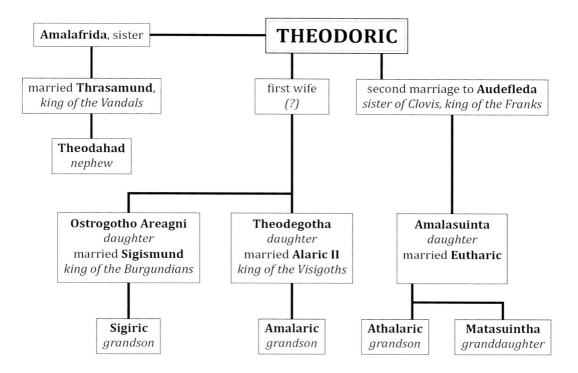

Theodoric's family tree.

in Spain, the Visigothic royal treasure was taken to Ravenna, and Theodoric's administration took control of taxation in the Visigothic kingdom.

Theodoric had not restored the old Western Empire but, presiding over a pan-Gothic regime and with wider family alliances, he looked more and more like a successor to the Western Roman emperors.

Religious Schisms

Relations with the Church were complicated by the theological disputes and heresies that characterised the early centuries of Christianity. As we have seen, the Goths were Arians—followers of Arius of Alexandria who maintained that Jesus was created by God and thus separate from (or not of the same substance as) God. This view had been branded heretical back in 325 by the Ecumenical Synod Constantine had summoned at Nicaea. The Nicene Creed states firmly that Christ and God are of the same substance. In the fourth century, Arian beliefs were still held by distinguished

Romans, including the Emperors Constantius II and Valens, but in the fifth century, the orthodox teaching was consolidated, and Arianism largely confined to barbarians.

However, that was by no means the end of Church disputes about Christ's divinity. In the fifth century, the Archbishop of Constantinople, Nestorius, argued that within Christ there were two persons, one divine and one human, and that Mary gave birth to a man. This doctrine, Nestorianism, was condemned at an Ecumenical Council convened by Theodosius II in 431 as over-emphasising the human side of Christ. The orthodox view was that Christ was a single person, at once both God and Man. Soon afterwards another school of thought asserted that the human nature of Christ was completely absorbed within the divine and therefore that Christ was of one nature only (Monophysite). The Ecumenical Council convened by Emperor Marcian at Chalcedon in 451 condemned Monophysitism as heresy too, affirming that Christ had two natures unified within one person.

As an Arian ruler of an Arian people, Theodoric did his best to remain aloof from these disputes. This became difficult, however, when doctrinal differences emerged between Constantinople and Rome. The Council of Chalcedon may have condemned Monophysitism but it did not succeed in exterminating it. It lingered in Alexandria and found some sympathy in Constantinople, where in 482, the Patriarch Acacius and Emperor Zeno had produced a compromise document, the *Henotikon*, which aimed to reconcile the Chalcedonians and the Monophysites and to sidestep the question of one or two natures. This was done without consulting Rome. The Pope was a Chalcedonian who disputed the document and excommunicated Acacius, triggering the Acacian schism.[8]

Zeno's successor as Eastern emperor, Anastasius, initially withheld his recognition of Theodoric in an attempt to pressure Rome into accepting the *Henotikon*, finally legitimising him in 496. At that point, he expected agreement by a new Pope. However, that Pope then died and his successor, Pope Symmachus, remained hostile to the *Henotikon*. A rival Pope, Laurentius, more sympathetic to Constantinople, was then elected, and thus began the Laurentian schism. Theodoric could no longer stay completely above the battle: he had to decide which Pope he would deal with and he backed Symmachus. The east–west schism was only finally healed in 519 after the death of Emperor Anastasius, since his successor, Justin, was a strict Chalcedonian.

Throughout this period, the Goths remained staunch Arians. Arianism was a mark of their separate and distinctive identity.

Arian Church-Building

As in effect the head of the Arian Church, Theodoric took his religious responsibilities seriously. He appointed Arian bishops; he had the Gothic translation of the Gospels made by Ulfilas written on purple parchment in silver ink; and, above all, he built churches.[9] He gave Ravenna an Arian cathedral on the site of what later became the church of St Theodore and, in the fifteenth century, the church of Santo Spirito, then, beside it, the Arian baptistery that stands today as a World Heritage site, preserving a charmingly rich mosaic.

The baptistery is an octagonal structure with apses, built of brick. It has sunk into the ground over the centuries and was originally higher and surrounded by an ambulatory. In the interior, only the cupola is decorated. At its centre is a portrayal of Christ's baptism by John the Baptist surrounded by an outer ring of apostles.

Conceptually, this is similar to the central feature of the Neonian Baptistery but much simpler. The positions of John the Baptist and the elderly man representing the Jordan River have been reversed. The Jordan River figure is much more prominent than in the Neonian portrayal and has a pair of lobster claws on his head. Experts have debated whether the pictorial differences between the two baptisteries show evidence of the doctrinal differences between Arianism and orthodox Catholicism and commented on the Gothic fashion of a moustache without a beard on one of the apostles in the Arian baptistery. However, the representation of Christ's baptism was preserved unaltered when the Arian baptistery was reconsecrated as an orthodox Catholic oratory in 561 after the fall of the Ostrogothic regime.

Theodoric's greatest Arian church was the Basilica built next to what is believed to have been his palace.[10] Since the ninth century, this church has been known as Sant'Apollinare Nuovo, following the transfer here in 856 of some St Apollinaris relics from Sant'Apollinare in Classe.[11] It would have been known in Theodoric's time as the Church of the Saviour or the Church of Christ. According to a later source, an inscription in the apse read: 'King Theodoric had this church built from its foundations and dedicated it to the name of Jesus Christ our Lord'.[12]

Sant'Apollinare Nuovo was constructed of brick in a simple basilica shape. The bell tower was a later addition. Its glory is the mosaic decoration of its interior. Two rows of twelve columns create a long central nave and lead to an apse. The original apse has been destroyed, as has much of the original decoration but the mosaics on the nave walls remain to be admired fifteen centuries later.

The wall mosaics are in three tiers. On the top band are twenty-six scenes from the life of Christ, the north wall telling the story of his teaching and miracles and the south wall representing the Passion and Resurrection. The middle zone has images of white-robed prophets, holding scrolls and books. The lowest tier includes very unusual secular images to be found in a church: mosaic portrayals of the city of Ravenna, of Theodoric's palace, and of Ravenna's port at Classe, which demonstrate Theodoric's pride in his capital and his ability to place his own secular images in a religious building.

The original decoration of Sant'Apollinare Nuovo in Theodoric's time was overlaid in places during the reign of Justinian when the church-building was reconsecrated in the name of St Martin as an orthodox Catholic church. The line of twenty-six male saints led by St Martin dates from this time. So does the procession of female martyrs led by three rather lively *magi* with red Phrygian caps.

Some figures portrayed in alcoves in the mosaics of Theodoric's palace were excised after the re-consecration, leaving images of unattached hands lingering to tell the tale. This suggests that members of the Ostrogoth royal family may have been portrayed

Above: Arian Baptistery. (*claudio zaccherini/Shutterstock.com*)

Below: Arian Baptistery, cupola. (*futureGalore/Shutterstock.com*)

Sant'Apollinare Nuovo, Classe ships. (*Inguaribile Vlaggiatore/Shutterstock.com*)

Sant'Apollinare Nuovo. (*Comune of Ravenna*)

Sant'Apollinare Nuovo, line of male saints. (*Alvaro German Vilela/Shutterstock.com*)

Sant'Apollinare Nuovo, the Magi mosaic. (*vvoe/Shutterstock.com*)

here and, as Arian heretics, could no longer be left there when the church was converted to orthodox Catholicism. A portrait labelled Justinian on the west wall has invited speculation that the face is actually Theodoric's with a name change.[13]

Archiepiscopal Chapel

While Theodoric presided over Arian church-building, the orthodox Catholic church, with its own line of bishops, was free to build for itself and did so. The archiepiscopal chapel, also known as St Andrew's Chapel, was built as a private oratory for the bishops during the time of bishop Peter II (494–520).

It was a brick structure, in shape not unlike the Mausoleum of Galla Placidia but with a semi-circular apse opposite the entrance hall. A lunette above the entrance portrays Christ as a warrior trampling on a lion and a serpent. The text of the book facing outwards ('*Ego sum via, veritas et vita*' from the Gospel of St John) is thought to have had anti-Arian connotations.

Above the vaulted main chapel at the centre is a medallion with Christ's monogram, held up by four angels shown with the symbols of the four Gospel writers. The arches around the vault are studded with medallions portraying martyrs and apostles. The decoration is testimony to the Ostrogothic kingdom's ability to have highly skilled mosaic artists working in parallel in both orthodox Catholic and Arian churches.

Archiepiscopal chapel. (*Comune of Ravenna*)

Amalasuinta

Theodoric was succeeded on his death, as he had wished, by his grandson Athalaric, now aged ten, whose mother, Amalasuinta, acted as regent. However, holding together Italy's Romano-Goth political union now became more difficult.

The Romans went through three phases in their relationship with their Gothic invaders. When, early in the fifth century, the Visigoths attacked Italy and sacked Rome, they were viewed as a threat and hated. Roman authors have given us scornful descriptions of their 'coarse ignorant brutish habits' and the 'fetid odour' of their bodies and garments. However, under Odoacer and, more significantly, under the Ostrogoths, the Romans of Italy had enjoyed conditions of relative peace and prosperity. They continued to feel socially superior but acknowledged that it was barbarian rulers who were upholding the Roman laws that protected their property.

Now there was a new factor. During the reign of Eastern Emperor Anastasius, Rome and Constantinople had been estranged over religious doctrine, but Justin had ended the schism by returning the Eastern Empire to Chalcedonian orthodoxy and it was now less obvious to the Romans that Italy's future lay with the next generation of Arian Ostrogoths.

Nor were the Gothic nobles all convinced that Theodoric's young grandson was a preferable successor to his adult nephew, Theodahad; some were restless under this two-nation state, feeling that the culture and character of the Goths was being suppressed by Romanisation.

Amalasuinta sought to maintain the Roman ethos of the regime. She tried to bring up her son within the Roman educational culture. Here, however, she faced opposition from Gothic courtiers who scorned Roman schools because the boys there could have their manhood insulted by being caned. They prized fighting and drinking above philosophy and rhetoric. Despite her efforts, Athalaric grew up a dissolute drunkard.

Amalasuinta was also careful to stay close to Constantinople. Justin died in 527 and was succeeded by his nephew Justinian, who had already been elevated to the status of co-emperor. She held to Theodoric's carefully nourished fiction that the Ostrogothic kingdom represented the Eastern emperor in Italy. When she detected a Gothic plot against her, Amalasuinta secured an assurance from Justinian that, if necessary, she could find sanctuary and asylum in the Eastern Empire. She even despatched a shipload of treasure to Constantinople in anticipation of having to flee. With this option in reserve, she organised the assassination of the three principal ringleaders of the conspiracy.

However, in 534, Athalaric died as a result of his dissipation and Amalasuinta's position became untenable. Reluctantly, she turned to Theodahad, with whom she was on bad terms, having as Regent curbed his illegal confiscation of property. She now proposed that Theodahad be invested with the title of king provided she could continue to rule. Theodahad agreed but promptly double-crossed her. He threw her into prison on an island where, with his connivance, she was murdered by relatives of the conspirators she had assassinated.[15]

The murder of Amalasuinta was the trigger, and the pretext, for Justinian's decision to invade Italy. His 'reconquest' was to be prolonged by civil war and it would be 552 before the Ostrogoths were finally expelled from Italy, but it is with Amalasuinta's death and Theodahad's brief reign that the Romano-Gothic regime founded by Theodoric really came to an end. It had been a prodigious feat of political balance. Even in its twilight years, it continued to sustain Ravenna's church-building. It was during Amalasuinta's regency that the orthodox Catholic Church began construction of the last two of the city's eight World Heritage monuments.

Byzantine Ravenna

Although the Western Roman Empire had disintegrated during the fifth century, the Eastern Roman Empire was to survive until the fifteenth, when the Ottoman Turks finally conquered Constantinople. In the Middle Ages, when all connection with Italy had been lost, the Eastern Roman Empire became in effect Greek but in the sixth century, during the reign of Justinian, it was still the Latin-speaking New Rome. We may call Justinian (527–565) a Byzantine emperor but, like his contemporaries and his successors, he called himself a Roman.

Justinian

There are two very different ways of looking at Emperor Justinian's relationship to Ravenna. The first is of a very positive commitment. In reconquering Italy, Justinian restored the undivided Roman Empire. He rescued Italy from a failing and fractious divided Ostrogoth regime, returned the Romans to Roman rule, suppressed Arianism, and restored orthodox Catholic Christianity. He had a warm relationship with the Church in Ravenna and promoted bishop Maximian to be an archbishop. Some of the finest Ravenna churches were constructed during his reign, notably San Vitale and Sant'Apollinare in Classe, and Justinian and Empress Theodora are deservedly represented in mosaic panels in the apse of San Vitale.

The other perspective is of Justinian mainly focused on the Eastern Empire, particularly on the recurring conflict with Persia. In trying to restore the Western Roman Empire at the same time, he almost bankrupted his government. He seriously under-resourced his generals in the west. This subjected Italy to a prolonged and destructive civil war for a reconquest that was swiftly overturned by the Lombards after his death. Neither he nor Theodora ever visited Ravenna and, while San Vitale and Sant'Apollinare in Classe were consecrated during his reign, their original construction began under the Ostrogoths. In ending Ostrogoth rule, he destroyed a valuable cultural bridge between the Romans and the most civilised of the barbarians. Indeed, he may even have recognised this danger, having been willing to see an Ostrogoth kingdom survive in north Italy.

Emperor Justinian. (*Petar Milošević, own work, CC BY-SA licence*)

A rounded picture of Justinian needs to encompass aspects of both these perspectives and to recognise the complexity of his character. He was deeply Christian and keen to suppress any residual paganism. An edict of 529 prohibited the traditional teaching of philosophy in Athens in the empire. Periodically, pagans were arrested, and their books publicly burned. Justinian was also preoccupied with theology. He was hostile to Arianism and wished to stamp out from its barbarian adherents in the west the heretical belief that Jesus was separate from, and not of the same substance as, God. He was determined to uphold Chalcedonian orthodoxy (that Christ combined both human and divine natures in one person), though willing to appease Miaphysites (moderate Monophysites who emphasised Christ's divine nature) in order to avoid an outright sectarian split.

His most famous domestic achievement was his codification of Roman law. He was also an ambitious builder, quick to rebuild central Constantinople in the aftermath of the destructive riots of 532 during which he reportedly lost his nerve and nearly fled. The Great Palace and the Senate House were burned and had to be replaced and so did the cathedral of St (Hagia) Sophia. The new Hagia Sophia, which in repaired form still stands today, with its huge dome, enormous space, marble columns, and mosaic decoration, was a wonder of its age. In all, Justinian built, or rebuilt, thirty-five churches in Constantinople, embodying in stone his fierce commitment to strengthening orthodox Christianity. He presided over church construction across the empire and even sent out ships with prefabricated marble church interiors to sites in Italy and North Africa.

In foreign policy too, Justinian was bold and ambitious, unafraid to spend from the well-filled treasury which had been bequeathed by Anastasius. At the start of his reign, Justinian faced east. He had inherited a war against the Persian King Kavadh. However, Kavadh's death in 531 offered the possibility of a peace treaty with his successor Khusro (also known as Chosroes). It was termed an 'Eternal Peace' after Justinian paid Khusro 11,000 gold pounds. This gave Justinian the opportunity to turn to the west.

His first concern here was the province of Africa, centred on Carthage. The Vandals had deposed a king who favoured closer relations with the Eastern Empire and replaced him with a more militant Arian called Gelimer. Justinian despatched 600 ships, 5,000 cavalry, and 10,000 infantry, many of them Huns, to reconquer the province. They were commanded by his leading general, Belisarius, whose life's work is interwoven with Justinian's (and is retold in a fictitious biography by Robert Graves). Belisarius achieved a remarkable victory in 533, the Vandals proving no match for the Huns. He recaptured Carthage, overthrew the long-standing Vandal kingdom, and restored Africa to orthodox Catholicism. Belisarius returned to Constantinople with the captive Vandal Gelimer to enjoy a traditional Roman triumph, while Justinian's mind turned to the Arian kingdom of Italy.

The Reconquest of Italy

The Byzantine invasion of Africa had been supported by Amalasuinta, the empire's Ostrogoth ally, who provided food and supplies in Sicily for Belisarius's expedition. Whether Justinian would have invaded Italy but for Amalasuinta's murder is unclear. He might have been willing to continue for a period the fiction that the Ostrogothic king was an imperial viceroy and perhaps hoped that Amalasuinta might help him bring Italy back into the empire without the need for war. However, Justinian must have been impressed by the ease with which Africa had been reconquered and Theodahad's murder of Amalasuinta now determined him to invade Italy.

In 536, Justinian launched two forces against Theodahad, one by land through Dalmatia and the other, led by Belisarius, by sea to attack Sicily. He encouraged the Franks to attack too. The Goths killed the general leading the Dalmatian expedition and halted its progress. Belisarius's army was much smaller than the one he had led against the Vandals, but he soon conquered Sicily and crossed to the Italian mainland. Belisarius then fought his way north and, after a three-week siege, captured Naples.

The Byzantine success prompted the Goths to depose Theodahad, who had made no effort to come to the help of Naples. They elected an elderly general named Witigis as their new king. Witigis promptly killed Theodahad. However, he decided not to try to defend Rome at this point. Instead, he withdrew to Ravenna to pay off the Franks. There, he forcibly married Amalasuinta's daughter, Matasuintha, in an attempt to establish some kind of hereditary legitimacy for his rule.

Belisarius proceeded to Rome and was welcomed into the city by the Pope and by its citizens. The Romans were ambivalent about his arrival. On the one hand, the army entering Rome called itself a Roman army. Belisarius and the Byzantines were supposedly kith and kin. However, the Eastern Empire had been a separate entity for more than a century and was increasingly seen as Greek. Moreover, many of the troops in the Byzantine army were barbarians who had rampaged through Naples after its capture. The Romans valued the peace that the Ostrogoths had given them and, most of all, they wanted to avoid a destructive period of conflict.

They were soon disabused of any such hope. In 537, Witigis returned south with an enlarged force and besieged Belisarius in Rome, trapping him there and starving the city's population for more than a year. Roman loyalties were torn. Belisarius suspected the Pope of intriguing with the Goths, deposed him and appointed his successor. Finally, imperial reinforcements changed the balance of strength, forcing the Goths to withdraw and enabling Belisarius to return to the attack.

The Byzantines then advanced north through Italy. Towns were captured, siege by siege, but at a high price: central Italy was devastated by famine. In Picenum, 50,000 farmers are believed to have died. In 538, a small Byzantine force was welcomed into Milan but a large Gothic army, reinforced by 10,000 Burgundian allies, soon surrounded the city and began to starve it into submission. Belisarius's relationship with his leading commanders had deteriorated and they were unable to coordinate an effective relief expedition. Milan fell to the Goths, who killed all the male inhabitants of the city and presented the women as captives to the Burgundians.

Finally, Belisarius managed to push Witigis and his army back into Ravenna, but its natural defences prevented its outright capture. Instead, Belisarius had to mount a siege but both sides recognised a stalemate. As a long shot, Witigis sent a letter to the Persian King Khusro, urging him to attack Constantinople, but meanwhile, he despatched ambassadors to the emperor with a brief to negotiate.

Justinian was concerned about the Persian threat and willing to agree terms with the Goths. In the circumstances, his offer was a generous one. Witigis could continue to be king of the Ostrogoths but in a much-reduced kingdom confined to Italy north of the river Po. Here he could be an imperial ally and buffer against potential incursions into Italy by the Franks or the Lombards. The Goths insisted that the agreement be signed by Belisarius since his army was encamped around their city. However, Belisarius refused to sign: he had invested four years in recapturing Italy from Witigis and he wanted now to complete the reconquest.

The Goths then changed tack. In 540, they offered Belisarius the throne of Italy: not only could he restore the Western Roman Empire, he could become its emperor. Aware that it had proved much easier in the past to conquer Ravenna by subterfuge than by force, Belisarius feigned agreement to this proposal. He was therefore invited to enter Ravenna peacefully with his own troops. He then captured Witigis and revealed the deceit. There was no looting and no killing. Belisarius was proud of his cunning bloodless victory and of the loyalty he had shown to Justinian. He returned to Constantinople with Witigis and other Gothic nobles as his prisoners and looked forward to another triumphant victory parade through the capital.

The celebration, however, was muted. Belisarius had not only defied Justinian's strategic judgment, he had also masqueraded as a Roman emperor. Moreover, as Justinian had feared, the Persian King Khusro broke the 'Eternal Peace' that same year. He captured Antioch, set it ablaze, and then attacked a series of other cities, which he ransacked for gold and treasure. Belisarius was despatched to the east to shore up the campaign against him.[1]

Plague and Warfare

In 541–542, the eastern Mediterranean was hit by bubonic plague. Justinian himself fell victim to it but recovered. Around 10,000 people reportedly died each day in Constantinople during this period. In the midst of the epidemic, the city also suffered an earthquake. Across the whole region, the plague was similar in scale to the Black Death in the fourteenth century and the empire lost a significant proportion of its population, perhaps as much as 20–25 per cent. Procopius tells us that too few were left living to bury the dead. Agriculture was severely damaged, cities shrank in size, tax revenues shrivelled, and warfare was disrupted. Khusro retreated but conflict continued until a truce was agreed in 545.

Meanwhile, the Goths had found themselves a formidable new leader, Totila, who was determined to end the Byzantine occupation of Italy. In 542, he marched into central and southern Italy and captured a host of cities including Naples. He fought not just to defeat Justinian's generals but also to win back the loyalty of the Romans to Ostrogoth rule. He promised the poor an end to exploitation by Justinian's tax-gatherers and undertook to liberate slaves. In 545, laying siege to Rome, he appealed to the Senate to remember the benefits Ostrogoth rule had given them in the days of Theodoric and Amalasuinta.

Belisarius was sent back to Italy but with an inadequate number of troops for the challenge he now faced. This was partly due to Justinian's prioritisation of the Persian front, partly to the difficulty of recruiting soldiers following the ravages of the plague. In 546, Totila entered Rome where he summoned the Senate and reproached it for deserting the Ostrogoth regime. He sent an embassy to Justinian in Constantinople, recalling the peace and prosperity of Theodoric's rule under the aegis of the Eastern Empire, adding 'If this should be also your desire, I shall look upon you as my father'.[2] His offer was rejected and he then faced a dilemma over what to do next. Since he wanted to rule over the Romans, he heeded Belisarius's plea not to burn and destroy their ancient capital. Instead, he evicted most of its population and then withdrew.

Belisarius was subsequently able to re-enter and re-populate Rome, but there was little else he could do to defeat Totila. In 548, he sent his wife, Antonina, a close friend of Empress Theodora (and, like her, a former actress and prostitute), back to Constantinople to use her influence to secure additional troops. However, Antonina found that Theodora had just died and, shorn of her ally, gave up her mission. Instead, she persuaded Justinian to recall Belisarius.

Fighting in Italy continued. In 549, Totila subjected Rome to yet another siege and took possession of it in 550. His troops also plundered Sicily. The small Byzantine force in Ravenna was powerless to stop the Gothic advances. The imperial reconquest of Italy had become an unresolved and destructive civil war.

Ravenna

It is hard to reconcile this picture of conflict and devastation during the 530s and 540s with arguably the greatest phase of church-building and decoration in Ravenna's history. The construction of San Vitale and Sant'Apollinare in Classe in particular were major projects extending over twenty years requiring investment, long-term commitment, and patient perseverance.

The investment was a special case. The Church certainly drew on generous donations from lay individuals but Julian the banker, also known as Julian the silversmith (*Julianus Argentarius*), was exceptional in the bountiful funding he provided for Ravenna's churches. He is believed to have spent 26,000 gold *solidi* on San Vitale alone and perhaps at least as much again on Sant'Apollinare in Classe and a small church called San Michele in Africisco (replicas of whose mosaics are now in a museum in Berlin). While many of Ravenna's earlier churches had been constructed with re-used bricks from older buildings, Julian is credited with paying for new bricks of a new shape.[3]

The social and economic conditions conducive to long-term commitment and perseverance, however, were the product of Ravenna's position during these two turbulent decades of warfare. Throughout the period, Ravenna, captured by trickery by Belisarius in 540, remained in imperial occupation. With its natural strong defences and its maritime communications with Constantinople, it managed to isolate itself from the mayhem that engulfed the rest of Italy. It even remained relatively prosperous, though it was hit by the plague in the 560s. As Byzantium's provincial capital and its safe Italian port, it was a bustling trading centre. Archaeological evidence suggests a flow of goods from the east. Marble from the island of Proconnesos and silks and spices from the orient were brought in by ship. Merchants, officials, clerics, and craftsmen could journey by land from Constantinople using the arterial *Via Egnatia* across Greece through Thessalonica to the Adriatic port of Dyrrachium and then by sea north to Ravenna. New arrivals partially compensated for the exodus of the Goths.[4]

As two of the city's greatest churches were completed in his reign, and because both he and his empress, Theodora, are represented in mosaic in San Vitale, Justinian is often given the credit for them. As we have seen, he was an energetic and ambitious builder of churches in Constantinople, but it is not clear whether the imperial Treasury provided any of the funding here. Justinian never visited Ravenna.

Justinian did, however, have a soft spot for Ravenna. This was an indirect result of his theological dabbling. As a staunch Chalcedonian, Justinian opposed the Miaphysites who emphasised the divine nature of Christ at the expense of the human side. However, Miaphysitism still flourished within the empire, especially in Egypt, and it was quietly supported by Empress Theodora.

Justinian wanted to win the Miaphysites over to Chalcedonian orthodoxy and he thought he could curry favour with them by taking a hard line against Nestorianism, which emphasised the human nature of Christ at the expense of the divine. He therefore issued an edict condemning the writings of three theologians who were deemed to display a Nestorian tendency. The edict was known as 'The Three Chapters'. He persuaded the patriarchs of Alexandria, Jerusalem, and Antioch to endorse it. The patriarch of Constantinople would only agree if the Pope did and, as it happened, the Pope was in Constantinople at the time and had his arm twisted. However, the edict was opposed by the bishops of north Italy. Apart from the Pope, somewhat under duress, only Ravenna aligned itself with the emperor.[5]

In 546, Justinian appointed an Istrian named Maximian as Ravenna's bishop and promoted him to the rank of archbishop. It fell to Maximian to consecrate the two great Ravenna churches which his predecessors had started and almost completed.

San Vitale

San Vitale had been commissioned by Bishop Ecclesius around 526 and its construction was undertaken, as well as funded, by Julian the banker. It was built on the site of an old temple where San Vitale was believed (probably falsely) to have been martyred. With no expense spared, it was architecturally complex and richly decorated. Huge quantities of marble must have been shipped in and the finest artists recruited from Constantinople and Rome. Its beautifully elaborate decoration was painstakingly completed, stone by stone, during the years when Totila and his troops were rampaging through Italy. Maximian completed it in 547–548.

Departing from the conventional Roman rectangular basilica shape, San Vitale has a Byzantine-style octagonal shape. It may well have been influenced by Constantinople church designs. Soaring pillars support a large cupola and give its central space strong vertical lines.

Its greatest magnificence lies in the gloriously coloured mosaic decorations of the sanctuary and of the apse within it. Entry is through an arch studded with medallions

San Vitale. (*claudio zaccherini/Shutterstock.com*)

portraying Christ, the apostles, and saints. On the side walls of the sanctuary are lunettes illustrating Old Testament scenes and, above them, episodes from the life of Moses and portraits of Jeremiah, Isaiah, and the four evangelists with their traditional symbols. The cross-vaulting of the sanctuary leads up to a white lamb of God with a halo surrounded by stars.

In the vault of the apse, a young and beardless Christ sits on a blue globe, from which the four rivers of Paradise flow into a pasture of flowers. On either side of Christ stands an archangel and, on the far left, San Vitalis. On the far right is Bishop Ecclesius, presenting Christ with a model of the church he founded.

On the side walls of the apse are perhaps the most famous mosaics of all: the two panels portraying the emperor and the empress. On the south side, Empress Theodora, richly dressed in a gown portraying the three Magi, and with a halo, is accompanied by her ladies-in-waiting who may include Belisarius's wife, Antonina, and their daughter.

On the north side, Justinian, bejewelled and with a halo, is the central figure in a group prominently including Maximian, who is named. Speculation surrounds the identity of the other figures: Belisarius might perhaps be next to Justinian, on his right, while the figure who seems to have been inserted behind the emperor and Maximian could perhaps be Julian the banker.

Above: San Vitale, sanctuary. (*UNESCO/copyright Aneta Ribarska*)

Below: San Vitale, apse. (*inavanhateren/Shutterstock.com*)

Above: San Vitale, Empress Theodora and entourage. (*mountainpix/Shutterstock.com*)

Below: San Vitale, Emperor Justinian and Archbishop Maximian. (*Samot/Shutterstock.com*)

San Vitale's completion was a high point in the Church's reassertion of orthodox Catholic doctrines after Ravenna's years under Arian domination. Bishop Ecclesius and his successors not only sought to rival and surpass the architecture and the decoration of the Arian churches built during the reign of Theodoric the Ostrogoth, but they also wanted their own imagery to counter the Arian heresy that Christ was not of the same substance as God, his creator. Prominent groups of three, found in several of San Vitale's mosaic illustrations, are thought to symbolise the Trinity, while allusions to St Paul's Epistle to the Hebrews are believed to point up a text implying the consubstantiality of God and his Son, which Arians rejected.[6]

Sant'Apollinare in Classe

Sant'Apollinare in Classe was constructed over broadly the same period as San Vitale. It lies 5 miles south of Ravenna in the old port. Its large brick basilica, to which a tall round bell tower was added in the tenth century, is visible from afar across the flat countryside on the city's outskirts.

The main basilica was commissioned by Bishop Ursicinus of Ravenna towards the end of the Ostrogoth regime and sited on an old burial ground. It was financed and built by Julian the banker and consecrated by Maximian in 549.

The width of the basilica is striking: its nave and two aisles almost look like three naves. Separating them are two fine rows of twelve columns of veined Greek marble topped by capitals decorated with 'acanthus leaves stirred by the wind'. The end wall at the east end forms a triumphal arch with a medallion of Christ's head at the centre. This is flanked by winged and haloed symbols of the four Gospel writers and beneath them two processions of sheep emerge from the cities of Jerusalem and Bethlehem. The arch decoration has undergone some alteration over the centuries.

The real glory of the church, however, lies in the sixth century mosaic decoration in the vault of the apse. In a representation of the Transfiguration of Christ on Mount Tabor, the hand of God points down from the sky to a star-studded disc containing a jewelled cross with a portrait of Christ's head at its centre. Moses and Elijah are in attendance as are three sheep representing the three disciples (Peter, James, and John) who were present at Mount Tabor.

Below the disc in the midst of the flowers, plants, pine trees, and rocks of the verdant landscape stands St Apollinaris himself, believed to have been Ravenna's first bishop, and twelve more sheep. In niches between the windows in the wall of the apse below the vault stand figures representing four of Ravenna's other distinguished bishops: Ecclesius, Severus, Ursus, and Ursicinus. In the seventh and eighth centuries, Sant'Apollinare in Classe became the burial place for Ravenna's bishops.

Above: Sant'Apollinare in Classe. (*Borisb 17/Shutterstock.com*)

Below: Sant'Apollinare in Classe, apse. (*Claudio Giovanni Colombo/Shutterstock.com*)

Sant'Apollinare in Classe, Bishops Ecclesius, Severus, Ursus, and Ursicinus. (*Author's collection*)

Leadership of the Bishops

The main driving force behind the construction of Ravenna's sixth century churches came from the bishops. The two World Heritage sites were not the only ones. Santa Maria Maggiore, adjacent to San Vitale and to the fifth century Santa Croce, was founded by Bishop Ecclesius. Bishop Victor enhanced the Ursiana cathedral. Maximian founded the church of St Stephen and restored the church of St Andrew. A church dedicated to Saints John and Paul and one to St Victor, and others in Classe, have also been identified from this period.

   The portrayal of Ravenna's bishops on church walls by Maximian is clear signification of their leadership in the church-building. As we have seen, Bishop Ecclesius is shown in the apse of San Vitale, in a group with Christ, two archangels and San Vitalis himself, offering a model of the church to Christ. In the group portrait on the side wall of San Vitale apse, Archbishop Maximian has not only placed himself alongside Emperor Justinian, he has also put himself at the front, judging from the position of his feet, and is the only named person in the group. Maximian was proud of the role of the bishops. He reportedly commissioned an altar cloth with images of all his predecessors and was probably instrumental in placing the figures of the four bishops on the east wall of Sant'Apollinare in Classe.[7]

Fifth and sixth century Bishops of Ravenna[8]

c. 405–431	Ursus
c. 431–450	Peter I Chrysologus
c. 450–473	Neon
c. 473–477	Expurantius
477–494	John I
494–520	Peter II
521	Aurelian
522–532	Ecclesius
533–536	Ursicinus
538–545	Victor
546–557	Maximian (Archbishops now)
557–570	Agnellus
570–578	Peter III
578–595	John II
595–606	Marinian

If the bishops, together with Julian the banker, deserve the main credit for the church-building and decoration which came to fruition in Ravenna during the Byzantine period, what is the significance of the portrayal of Justinian and Theodora within the sanctuary of San Vitale? As Justinian's appointee to the position of archbishop, Maximian was Justinian's closest clerical ally in Italy (the Pope's agreement to 'The Three Chapters' had proved fragile). Maximian must have either suggested the two mosaic panels to him and Theodora or, alternatively, sought their consent. Justinian would have readily agreed: what better way to proclaim to the citizens of Ravenna that they once again belonged to the Roman Empire? Moreover, like his Eastern Roman predecessors, Justinian saw himself as God's representative on earth and would have wanted to re-establish this concept in the west.

Imperial patronage of Maximian's archbishopric may or may not have extended to direct funding for church-building but it did have financial benefits. By keeping on good terms with Constantinople, the bishops of Ravenna were able to obtain tax benefits. The bishopric also received two imperial donations: one to Bishop Victor and a second to Bishop Agnellus. With the support of generous private donors as well, the diocese became rich.[9] Two features of its wealth, which were very probably imported from Constantinople, are the intricately carved ivory throne of Maximian, now in the Archiepiscopal Museum in Ravenna, and the magnificent marble ambo (pulpit) of his successor Agnellus, a sixth-century feature in the eighteenth-century rebuilt cathedral.

Justinian's Final Years

Meanwhile, except in Ravenna and three other isolated cities, the Ostrogoths had established control. Symbolically, Totila had taken up residence in Rome, which he had recaptured in 550 and where he now disported himself as Italy's ruler. He reopened the Senate, aiming to reconstitute it with both Ostrogoth and Italo-Roman members. He also restored Games to the Circus Maximus where he graced the imperial box.

At last, Justinian decided to take effective action to bring the Italian war to a close. He appointed his cousin, and perhaps potential heir, Germanus, as commander of a new invasion force. Germanus was now married to Theodoric's grand-daughter Matasuintha (freed from her earlier unhappy marriage by Witigis's death). Justinian hoped that this couple, linking the imperial and Ostrogothic dynastic lines, would provide a rule in Italy acceptable to Romans and Goths alike. It was an ambitious plan for a statesmanlike peace but, before it could be implemented, Germanus died.

For a new general, Justinian turned to an Armenian eunuch called Narses, who had fought in Italy much earlier but had quarrelled with Belisarius and been recalled. He was now in his eighties. Narses insisted on having a large army and he marched into northern Italy at the head of 30,000 troops, 5,000 of whom were Lombards. He confronted Totila in the Apennines at a historic site called *Busta Gallorum*, the Tomb of the Gauls, and defeated him. Totila was killed in flight. The Goths fought on but Narses beat them again in a battle south of Naples, killing their new king, Teias. After this, the Goths surrendered and in 552 agreed to leave Italy. By then, a Frankish force had invaded Italy from the north but Narses defeated it too. Italy was finally restored to the empire.

In 554, Justinian imposed civilian order throughout the country by issuing a Pragmatic Sanction, overturning Totila's decisions but upholding the policies of Amalasuinta, Athalaric, and Theodahad. Troublesome Goths were deported. Property taken illegally under Totila was to be returned to its owners. The administrative role of bishops was extended. Arian churches were closed or reconsecrated as orthodox Catholic churches. In Ravenna Sant'Apollinare Nuovo, built and decorated as an Arian palace chapel by Theodoric the Ostrogoth, was transformed into an orthodox Catholic church dedicated to St Martin, with new mosaic panels, some doctoring of the Arian mosaics, and the addition of a portrait of Justinian. The Arian Baptistery became an oratory dedicated to the Virgin Mary. With its glorious new churches of San Vitale and Sant'Apollinare in Classe as well, Byzantine Ravenna now eclipsed Ostrogoth Ravenna.

Justinian must have thought that he had finally reunited the old Roman Empire and, for the time being, so he had. As well as clearing the Ostrogoths out of Italy, he had regained the province of Africa from the Vandals, albeit with periodic frontier threats from the Berbers.

In 552, he even managed, through opportunism, to win back a toehold in southern Spain by intervening in a dynastic dispute among the Visigoths and established a small new Byzantine province there.

However, the frontiers of Justinian's restored Roman Empire were as fragile as ever. The Persians were only kept at bay by the payment of subsidies the imperial treasury could no longer easily afford. Slav invaders attacked the Balkans in 548 and 550. A tribe of Kutrigur Bulgars penetrated even further in 559, plundering Thrace and threatening Constantinople. Justinian brought Belisarius out of retirement to confront them but peace was secured by the payment of a subsidy, not by military victory.

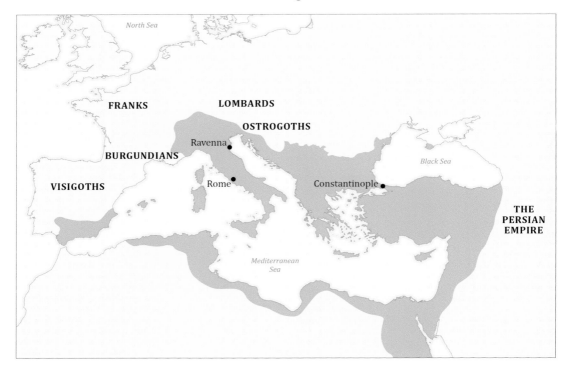

Map of the Roman empire at the time of Justinian's death, AD 565.

Constantinople was again hit by a major earthquake in 557, causing the dome of Hagia Sophia partially to collapse. In 558, the plague returned. Food shortages and a drought led to recurrent outbreaks of street violence. The ageing emperor was increasingly preoccupied with his theological disputes, neglecting both the economy and the empire's military defence. In 565, Justinian died, aged eighty-three.[10]

It had taken Justinian sixteen years to complete the reconquest of Italy and the protracted civil war had inflicted devastation and destruction on the peninsula. His Italian legacy, outside Ravenna, was a wrecked economy and a broken society. Justinian is often blamed for destroying the Ostrogoth regime that had uniquely integrated Romans and barbarians while upholding Roman institutions and culture, and that had provided a period of more than forty years of peace after the fall of the Western Empire.

Although restoring the undivided Roman Empire was an overriding ambition, on two occasions Justinian had seemed willing to contemplate a continuing Ostrogoth contribution to his rule. The first was in the set of terms he offered Witigis in 539 when Belisarius was besieging him in Ravenna. The second was when he sent Germanus and his Ostrogoth wife, Matasuintha, to Italy in 550, hoping they might create an Italy that would assimilate the Goths peacefully into the empire. However, the first initiative was stymied by Belisarius's determination to complete the military reconquest of Italy by subterfuge, while the second was frustrated by Germanus's untimely death. Justinian may not therefore have been wholeheartedly set on exterminating the Ostrogoth regime, though in the event that is what he did.

However, the Byzantine victory soon unravelled. Only three years after Justinian's death, the Lombards invaded Italy and a prolonged Byzantine-Lombard war followed. By the end of the sixth century, the Lombards had gained control of two-thirds of Italy.

Ravenna, however, remained in Byzantine hands. Narses became its governor, becoming a forerunner of the later Byzantine Exarchs who combined both military and civilian authority. They ruled a shrinking Italian province, but a splendidly endowed city, from their home in Theodoric's Ravenna palace.

An Exceptional Case

Ancient Ravenna reached its cultural apogee in the mid-sixth century, when the Byzantine churches of San Vitale and Sant'Apollinare in Classe were added to the legacy from the Ostrogoth and late western imperial periods. This was arguably when social and economic conditions in the rest of Italy had reached their nadir. The fall of the Western Empire and the regime changes that followed had ended, after an interlude of peace under the Ostrogoths, in a destructive civil war with sieges of Italy's cities, economic devastation of the countryside, impoverishment, famine, and depopulation. Ravenna's great heritage stayed largely intact.

We set out to answer the question of how Ravenna's splendid art and architecture could have been created during such turbulent times. How could investment and commitment requiring stability and security have been sustained amid the turmoil? Chapter 2 identified three strands of continuity that provide the themes of the explanation: the success of the Church in detaching itself from the falling Roman Empire; the extent to which the Goths became Romanised; and Ravenna's continuing role as a capital city under different regimes.

The narrative in Chapters 3–6 illustrated the interplay between these themes and political and military events. They suggest a fourth theme too: the growing significance of Ravenna's ties to the Eastern Empire. At the start of the fifth century, Ravenna was the capital of the Western Roman Empire; by the end of the sixth century, it had become an outpost of the Eastern Byzantine Empire.

The Church

The Church proved itself remarkably adaptable to changing circumstances during the period of the late Roman Empire. After Emperor Theodosius (379–395) made Christianity the imperial state religion and banned pagan sacrifices, the Church developed as a public institution in collaboration with the empire. To the Romans, the empire was synonymous with the civilised world; Christianity was now deemed to be the one true religion. These two concepts of universality almost became integrated.

Roman legal processes were used to stamp out paganism. The emperors claimed to be the Christian God's representatives on earth and took a keen interest in matters of theology, regarding it as their responsibility to cajole the Church leaders into doctrinal unity. The Church copied the secular Roman form of the basilica for the design of its churches. It also adopted the imperial organisational unit of the Diocese, which had been introduced by Diocletian for sub-divisions of a Province, producing a close alignment between religious and civil administrative divisions.

Yet the Church successfully kept itself semi-detached and, when Alaric the Goth sacked Rome in 410, St Augustine, as we have seen, spelled out the difference between the transience of the earthly city, identified with Rome, and the heavenly city where all Christian believers would find eternity. In the east, the close unity of Church and State continued and would shape relationships within the Byzantine empire. In the west, however, the Church smoothly established its own separate identity. It was hard to regard the emperors in Ravenna, Honorius and Valentinian III, let alone their successors Petronius Maximus, Avitus, Ricimer, Libius Severus, Anthemius, Olybrius, Glycerius, Julius Nepos, and Romulus Augustulus as God's representatives on earth.

Church organisation was based in the cities of the empire, with 'metropolitans' who had authority over a number of bishops. The Church leaders were the Pope, as bishop of Rome, and the Patriarchs of Constantinople, Antioch, Jerusalem, and Alexandria, but the individual bishops were also powerful figures. Within their dioceses, in addition to their spiritual duties, bishops took on broader administrative responsibilities and became increasingly important civic, as well as religious, leaders. As it grew in strength, the Church grew in wealth. Christ taught that it was hard for a rich man to enter the Kingdom of Heaven. The Church gave alms to the poor and encouraged the rich to believe that the path to salvation lay in making generous donations to the Church.

The early fifth century was a period of rapid growth for Christianity. Converts from paganism came to worship in large numbers and required baptism. Large basilica churches were constructed to respond to the demand. Interiors were decorated first with pastoral images of trees and plants but then, with increasing artistic ambition, with scenes from scripture, portrayals of martyrdom and stories from the life of Christ. Santa Maria Maggiore in Rome and San Lorenzo in Milan, like the churches of Ravenna, were intricately decorated in mosaic. Images were a vital means of communicating religious teachings to converts and worshippers with limited literacy.

In Honorius's Ravenna, Bishop Ursus (405–431?) founded the Ursiana cathedral, together with its adjacent baptistery. Under the next bishop, Peter Chrysologus (Peter I, 431–450), the Church benefited from the imperial patronage of Galla Placidia. Then it was Bishop Neon (450–473) who reconstructed and redecorated the Neonian Baptistery.

As the Western Empire began to crumble in the mid-fifth century, the Church was powerful enough and rich enough to distance itself from the state. It was able now to uncouple itself from the string of ineffectual emperors and military commanders who presided over its fall. It was untroubled by Odoacer's brief rule and soon found a *modus vivendi* with the Italian kingdom of Theodoric the Ostrogoth. While Theodoric built Arian churches, the bishops of Ravenna founded orthodox Catholic ones, constructing the Archiepiscopal chapel and laying the foundations for San Vitale and Sant'Apollinare in Classe.

With Justinian's reconquest of Italy, the Church adapted yet again and strengthened its relationship with the emperor in Constantinople. Bishop Maximian, promoted to Archbishop by Emperor Justinian, completed the decoration of San Vitale and Sant'Apollinare in Classe and incorporated portraits of Justinian and Theodora (and of himself) in the apse of San Vitale. Imperial patronage may or may not have extended to direct financial investment, but the main funding was provided by Julian the banker, and it is Bishop Ecclesius (522–532) who is portrayed as presenting the church of San Vitale to Christ. The Church deserves the main credit for the creation of Ravenna's fine art and architecture over the fifth and sixth centuries.

The Ostrogoths

We have seen that, while Romans used the term 'barbarians' to describe peoples outside the Roman Empire, in reality, there was no clear and tidy dividing line. Barbarians were inside, as well as outside, the empire. Some were invited in, some forced their way in, and, once inside, many became integrated into the Roman world, particularly into the Roman military.

The Ostrogoths were in a different category. They were not so much invited in as invited to invade. With Eastern Emperor Zeno's connivance and encouragement, their leader Theodoric was offered the opportunity to attack Italy and expel the barbarian Odoacer who had deposed the last Western emperor and made himself king.

Theodoric succeeded in creating a Romano-Gothic kingdom which brought a period of relative peace and stability to Italy. It was a regime of religious tolerance in which the Pope and the Church could feel comfortable. It provided an environment in which Roman and Byzantine architects and artists could, within their own cultural traditions, work in parallel on church-buildings for the Arian Goths and commissions from the bishops of Ravenna. Theodoric was the patron of the Arian cathedral and its Arian baptistery and constructed Sant'Apollinare Nuovo as his palace chapel. His daughter Amalasuinta, as Regent after his death, created the climate in which Bishop Ecclesius initiated the building of San Vitale and Bishop Ursicinus commissioned Sant'Apollinare in Classe.

In respect of art and architecture, the contrast between the Ostrogoth kingdom in Italy and the Visigoth kingdom in southern France and Spain is striking. The Visigoth kingdom was established, initially in Aquitaine, before the final fall of the Western Empire. As the imperial administration collapsed, Roman landowners reluctantly acknowledged the rule of these barbarians, because this was the only way of safeguarding their property and wealth. The Visigoth kings upheld Roman law, continued a form of Roman tax gathering, and appointed Romans to civilian office:

during the 470s, Leo of Narbonne, for example, became the chief adviser to the Visigoth King Euric. Alaric II, Euric's son, produced a legal code modelled on, and largely drawn from, imperial legislation. The Visigoths thus developed a Romano-Gothic regime before either Odoacer or Theodoric the Ostrogoth. The Visigoth kings also preserved good relations with the orthodox Catholic Church, while creating their own Arian dioceses in Narbonne, Barcelona, Toledo, and elsewhere. Yet there is no legacy of religious art and architecture from the Visigoth kingdom remotely comparable to that of Ravenna.

The Visigoths lacked the stability of the Ostrogoth regime. Euric had succeeded to the Visigoth throne by killing a brother, as indeed that brother had previously done himself. At the end of the fifth century the Visigoths were driven out of Gaul by the Franks, whose King Clovis became a baptised Catholic and to whom the Roman aristocracy started to shift their allegiance. However, it was not just the Visigoth kingdom that the Ostrogoths surpassed in art and architecture. When the Frankish kingdom evolved over later centuries into the early Holy Roman Empire, it was to Ravenna that Charlemagne (742–814) turned for inspiration. He carried off building materials from Theodoric's palace and an equestrian statue of Theodoric and modelled his Palatine Chapel at Aachen on San Vitale. In the barbarian world, Ravenna's achievement was exceptional.

What made the Ostrogoth regime so special? It was, of course, based in Italy and in the former imperial capital and therefore drew strongly on Roman art and cultural traditions. The Ostrogoths had a close relationship with the Eastern emperors, whom Theodoric notionally represented and on whom Amalasuinta depended for support. Diplomatic and commercial contacts across the Adriatic to the Eastern Empire were constant, so Constantinople made its cultural influence felt in Ravenna.

However, an important part of the answer lies in Theodoric's personal qualities. He had been a well-treated hostage in Constantinople during his childhood (from the age of seven to the age of eighteen). He had had a Roman education and acquired an understanding of how to govern a Roman population as well as how to stay on good terms with the Eastern Roman emperors. He was therefore able to provide Italy with peace and relative prosperity over his long reign and, judging from the divisions which appeared within the Ostrogoth court after his death, it is clear that his own strength of personality held the Ostrogoth kingdom together.

Theodoric's Romano-Gothic kingdom has a major share, therefore, in the credit for Ravenna's artistic and architectural achievement.

Capital City Status

The third key factor behind Ravenna's cultural distinction was its capital city status, beginning with its adoption as the imperial residence for Emperor Honorius in 402. We saw in Chapter 3 how Rome was eclipsed from the time of Diocletian onwards, how Constantinople was created as the New Rome, and how it became the obvious capital for the Eastern emperors in the fifth century when the east and the west had separate rulers. However, in other circumstances, Milan could easily have become the capital of the Western Roman Empire. Emperor Honorius and his military commander Stilicho chose Ravenna because of its defensive and defensible character. Off to one side from the main route into central Italy, it shielded the emperor during the periods of invasion by Goths, Huns and Vandals when Milan and Rome were much more vulnerable. Had Honorius been a warrior emperor like his father Theodosius, however, he might well have chosen Milan as a better base from which to guard central Italy.

Ravenna's imperial role led to a scale and grandeur of palace and church-building that distinguished it from other cities. As the site of the emperor's residence, it warranted a cathedral and baptistery, which Bishop Ursus founded. Honorius's sister, Galla Placidia, then worked closely with the Church in founding San Giovanni Evangelista and Santa Croce, with its link to the chapel known as the Mausoleum of Galla Placidia.

Perhaps the key point, however, is that Ravenna retained a form of capital city status through the various regime changes, maintaining continuity of spending on prestigious buildings. Valentinian III left Ravenna for Rome towards the end of his reign and not all of his short-lived successors resided in Ravenna. However, Odoacer chose it as his regal capital. It was probably more acceptable to the Romans for their barbarian kings to be based in Ravenna than to reside in Rome. Theodoric then inherited Ravenna from Odoacer as his capital, creating Ravenna's great Arian church architecture and permitting building by the orthodox Catholic church as well.

Ravenna's defensive position explains its continuing role as a capital after the fall of the Western Empire. It was so impregnable that first Theodoric and then Belisarius only managed to occupy it by duping its defenders. During the lengthy and destructive Italian civil war in Justinian's reign, other cities underwent sieges and changed hands but Ravenna remained a safe base for the imperial side and became the natural provincial capital for Byzantine Italy. The Byzantine armies were unable to hold Rome or Milan during the decades of civil war, but they could maintain control of Ravenna.

Ravenna's magnificent churches, baptisteries and mausoleums can be ascribed therefore to the city's role as an imperial, regal, and then Byzantine provincial capital, all related to the fact that it was so militarily secure. Its continuing capital status gave it the prestige warranting the construction of major show-piece churches and monuments. Its nigh impregnable position, off the 'beaten track' during both the fifth-century barbarian invasions and the sixth-century Italian wars, shielded it and enabled its architects, builders, and mosaicists to work under conditions of relative peace and stability.

The Eastern Connection

Ravenna's connection to the Eastern Empire in Constantinople contributed to its architectural and artistic distinction in two ways: politically and artistically.

Politically, it lent the barbarian kingdom based in Ravenna a legitimacy that other barbarian regimes lacked. Odoacer had sought the blessing of the Eastern emperor for his kingship; Theodoric formally received it, having invaded Italy at the Eastern emperor's instigation in the first place. So, prior to Justinian's reign, Ostrogoth Italy with its capital at Ravenna carried a measure of imperial prestige which was reflected in the scale of the city's buildings.

Artistic influences also developed. In the early fifth century, the Western and Eastern halves of the empire had been consolidating their separation and the brothers Honorius and Arcadius were not close. The artistic tradition behind the design and decoration of Ravenna's churches, enjoying the patronage of Galla Placidia, was largely Roman. The Ostrogoths had a thriving trade with Constantinople and certainly imported building materials from the Eastern Empire and probably decorative ideas too. However, once Belisarius had captured Ravenna for the Byzantines, the political, commercial, and cultural links to Constantinople became much stronger.

As we have seen, Bishop Maximian was appointed by Justinian and Ravenna's church-building once again enjoyed imperial patronage, this time from the east. It was in this period that the architectural and artistic culture of Constantinople became most influential. Byzantine architects had great expertise in geometry and optics from which Ravenna almost certainly benefited.

The complex double-octagon structure of San Vitale (very different from the shape of Ravenna's other churches) closely resembles the design of the church of Saints Sergius and Bacchus in Constantinople. San Vitale was built between 526 and 547, Sts Sergius and Bacchus between 527 and 536. Some shared thinking on the design seems likely.[1]

When the Byzantine reconquest of Italy was completed, and the Arian churches of Ravenna were reconsecrated as orthodox Catholic places of worship, a difference in style can be seen. The Ostrogoth images in the upper tier of the nave of Sant'Apollinare Nuovo, simply telling the story of Christ's life, contrast with the stylised processions of saints and martyrs added in Justinian's reign. In identifying the factors that made Ravenna's experience and achievements unique, it is important to recognise the influence of the Eastern Empire, especially in the later period.

The Answer

We can now consolidate the answer to the question of how Ravenna's splendid art and architecture could have flourished during the turbulent conditions of the fifth and sixth centuries. In summary, the key factors were: the leadership of the bishops of Ravenna in the context of the Church's ability to adapt and detach itself from the falling Western Empire; the successful Romano-Gothic regime established by Theodoric the Ostrogoth, bringing a lengthy interlude of peace and religious tolerance; Ravenna's continuing role as a capital city under different regimes; and the city's ties to the Eastern Empire and the restoration of imperial patronage, this time from Constantinople, to which the bishops again adapted.

However, the explanation cannot be wholly couched in broad thematic terms. Would Ravenna have achieved such a high point of creativity in religious art and architecture had it not been for Honorius's lack of military ability, Theodoric's childhood as a hostage in Constantinople, or the generosity and commitment of Julian the banker? Elements of chance contributed to Ravenna's special circumstances.

When the Western Roman Empire collapsed, the experience was very different across Europe, province by province, and the degree to which Roman civilisation was assimilated by the various 'barbarians' varied. Italy, as we have seen, was different from the outer provinces because of the Romanisation of Theodoric and the Ostrogoths. Then, within Italy, Ravenna's experience was different from the rest of the peninsula, as a capital city, as an island of military security in times of invasion and civil war, and as an outpost of the Byzantine empire. In the turbulence of the fifth and sixth centuries, it was an exceptional case.

The Next Question

Looking at the eight World Heritage buildings in Ravenna today, a follow-up question arises. How did the churches and monuments of fifth and sixth century Ravenna manage to survive to become the UNESCO sites of today? The broad answer is that Ravenna succeeded in side-stepping some of the major risks of destruction that afflicted the wider Byzantine empire after Justinian's death.

The Lombard invasion of Italy began in 568. The Lombards came as settlers rather than as raiders and created their own Italian kingdom. They met very little resistance, but they made no attempt to capture Ravenna and its surrounding area, nor initially southern Italy and Sicily. Rome became an increasingly independent Papal state. Through protracted warfare over several decades, the Lombards expanded their territory, steadily reducing Byzantine Italy to a third of its original size. Pope Gregory I, ignoring Ravenna's exarch, made peace with the Lombards in 593.

By then, the Byzantine empire had far greater worries, as it came under attack from Persia in the east and from the Avars and Slavs in the Balkans. It was because of his inability to do much to help them that Emperor Maurice (582–602) had promoted the governors of Ravenna and Carthage to be exarchs with full military and civilian authority over their provinces. No sooner did Emperor Heraclius (610–641) rescue Byzantium from the Persians than Arab armies, enthused by their new religion of Islam, surged out of Arabia to conquer Persia and the Byzantine territories of Syria, Palestine, Egypt and North Africa. They penetrated Asia Minor and laid siege to Constantinople itself in 674 and again in 717.

Throughout all this, Ravenna's churches and monuments remained safe under the rule of its exarchs. For a period during the seventh century, the bishops of Ravenna became independent of the Pope, under a decree of Emperor Constans II, though this status did not last. Eventually, the city was captured by the Lombards in 751. They inflicted some damage, but their rule was brief. In 754, Pope Stephen II invited Pepin, king of the Franks, to expel them. It was in gratitude for this that Pope Hadrian I authorised Charlemagne to despoil Theodoric's palace. Ravenna was then governed by its own archbishops under the Papacy. The Popes looked to the Holy Roman Empire, rather than the Byzantine empire, for military protection, so Ravenna's link to Constantinople was broken for good.

This saved Ravenna's artistic heritage from another danger: iconoclasm. Interpretations of this phenomenon vary but the conventional explanation is that the Byzantines ascribed their disastrous defeats by the Arabs to the loss of God's favour and observed that Islam prohibited any form of idolatrous representation. Under Leo III (717–741) and, more seriously, under Constantine V (741–775), they started to destroy their own religious icons. In the church of the Virgin at Blachernae in Constantinople, for example, the emperor had the elaborate mosaic decorations portraying the life of Christ destroyed and replaced by scenes of flowers and birds. Iconoclasm was believed to have brought Constantine V military success against the Arabs, as he temporarily stabilised the empire's eastern frontier; fortunately, he failed to retain Ravenna.

A much greater threat to early Christian mosaic art, however, came directly from the Moslems (Arabs and Turks) whose invasions eventually destroyed the Byzantine empire. Islamic conquests extended from Asia Minor into Greece and the Balkans and from Africa to Spain and Sicily. Christian mosaics and frescoes were covered up or mutilated by hammer blows. Finally, in 1453, Constantinople itself fell to the Ottoman Turks. The mosaics of Haghia Sophia (or at any rate those left after Venetian plundering during the Fourth Crusade) were plastered over when the cathedral was converted into a mosque. With the exception of Sicily, however, Italy was spared an Islamic invasion.

Within Italy, Ravenna now lapsed into relative obscurity. Its port at Classe silted up and, as the sea receded, it ceased to be on the coast. It has been called a backwater, though this characterisation has been challenged by historians who have charted its reorientation northwards towards the Holy Roman Empire.[2] However, Venice became the leading maritime power in the Adriatic and indeed Ravenna was ruled by the Venetian Republic during much of the fifteenth century. It was not immune from periodic political and military conflicts, nor from floods and earthquakes, but essentially its comparative obscurity after the eighth century helped to preserve much of its great heritage.

Survival in What Form?

Ravenna's churches were much more successful in surviving than its palaces. All churches are subject to change, however. Some are augmented, some rebuilt in a different style, others restored, towers may be added, the ground level can alter: the religious buildings of Ravenna were no exception. Their survival has ultimately to be explained case by case.

In the imperial era, Galla Placidia's name is closely associated with three buildings in particular: San Giovanni Evangelista, Santa Croce, and her Mausoleum. San

Giovanni Evangelista, which once housed the mosaic recounting the shipwreck and salvation of Galla Placidia and her children, was reconstructed more than once and is now a largely modern church, rebuilt after it was accidentally bombed during the Second World War. Santa Croce survived in broadly its original form until the end of the fourteenth century when it began to be dismantled and this process was completed in 1602: today, its shell is an excavation site. Galla Placidia's Mausoleum, which was originally attached to Santa Croce, was the exception in surviving intact. Even so, the marble floor was restored in the sixteenth century, when the floor level was raised, and a yellow Siena marble lining to the walls was added during a phase of restoration at the end of the nineteenth century.

The principal church built by the bishops during the imperial period was the Ursiana Cathedral, to which a bell tower was added in the tenth century. However, the cathedral was demolished in 1733 and completely replaced by the current *Duomo*. The baptistery attached to the original cathedral, as we have seen, was reconstructed and redecorated by Bishop Neon to become the Neonian Baptistery. Here too, the floor level was raised during some extensive work carried out in the twelfth century. Restoration work on the mosaics in the dome was carried out in the period 1899 to 1906.

The new Arian cathedral built during the Ostrogoth period subsequently underwent a number of reincarnations. After the Justinian reconquest, it was reconsecrated and dedicated to St Theodore; in the eighth century, it housed a monastic community and was known as Santa Maria in Cosmedin; today, with a Renaissance portico added in 1543 and restoration following bomb damage in 1943, it is called Santo Spirito. It too had a baptistery attached which, while it has sunk by over 2 metres, survives—in state ownership since 1914—to display its mosaic-decorated cupola as the Arian Baptistery.

The alterations to the Arian basilica of Sant'Apollinare Nuovo did not end with the makeover it was given when it was reconsecrated as an orthodox Catholic church following Justinian's reconquest. The apse had to be reconstructed after an earthquake in the eighth century, a bell tower was added in the ninth or tenth century, the floor level was raised in the sixteenth century and a baroque apse was created. Significant restoration work was done on the mosaics in the 1850s and 1860s.

The Archiepiscopal Chapel, built by the orthodox Catholic Church during Theodoric's reign, was altered substantially during the sixteenth and seventeenth centuries. While much of its original mosaic decoration survives, the apse has been completely rebuilt. Theodoric's Mausoleum, though abandoned in the late middle ages, was rescued by restorers in more recent times.

From Byzantine Ravenna, Bishop Ecclesius's original church of Santa Maria Maggiore was largely rebuilt in a baroque style in 1671, while Maximian's St Stephen, known to us only from a written record, has disappeared. Only remnants have survived of Julian the banker's San Michele in Africisco. San Vitale had its porch replaced by a cloister in the tenth century; this cloister was replaced by a new one in the sixteenth, a bell tower was built in 1696, and the floor level raised. The cupola was decorated with a new set of frescoes in the baroque style in the eighteenth century and major restoration work was done on the mosaics at the end of the nineteenth century and into the twentieth. Sant'Apollinare in Classe had significant changes made to its original triumphal arch more than once, a crypt was built during the ninth century and a bell tower added in the tenth. Further change occurred in the eighteenth century and, again, major restoration work spanned the late nineteenth and early twentieth centuries.

While earlier building work may have been designed to reflect contemporary taste or simply to preserve the buildings as they were at the time, the ambitious programme which began at the end of the nineteenth century, spearheaded by Corrado Ricci, aimed to restore the monuments, where feasible, to their original forms—which required some (not uncontroversial) imagination.[3]

As an overview, we may say that Ravenna's descent into obscurity at the end of the eighth century helped preserve its monuments but, as this account shows, we have not inherited all of the finest art and architecture of the fifth and sixth centuries, nor is what we have inherited entirely what it once was.

Ravenna Today

Although 12 kilometres from the sea, Ravenna has now re-established itself as a port, thanks to a canal which was initially constructed during the eighteenth century. Docks and cargo terminals lie along the canal, as do shipyards. The port serves the province of Emilia-Romagna, supports a ferry service to Croatia and houses a large marina. It also provides a terminal for Adriatic cruise ships which call in to give their passengers the opportunity to visit the historic old city and its ancient churches and monuments.

In 1972, UNESCO (United Nations Educational, Scientific and Cultural Organisation) agreed a convention for the protection of the world's cultural and natural heritage. This involved identifying monuments, buildings, and sites of universal value worthy of international protection and establishing a fund to assist their conservation and, where appropriate, restoration.

The criteria for inclusion on the list included: representing a masterpiece of human creative genius; exhibiting an important interchange of human values, over a span of time or within a cultural area of the world, on developments in architecture or technology, monumental arts, town-planning or landscape design; bearing a unique or at least exceptional testimony to a cultural tradition or to a civilisation which is living or which has disappeared; and being an outstanding example of a type of building, architectural or technological ensemble or landscape which illustrates (a) significant stage(s) in human history.

In 1996, the eight early Christian monuments of Ravenna were inscribed in the World Heritage list on the basis that they conformed to these criteria.[4] The responsibility for protecting and managing the monuments still remains with the Italian state, Church and municipal authorities: the Ministry for Cultural Heritage

Above: Modern Ravenna, linked by canal to the sea. (*Giorgio Biserni*)

Below: Modern Ravenna, historic city centre. (*claudio zaccherini/Shutterstock.com*)

and Activities, the church Diocese, and the *Comune* (Municipality) of Ravenna. The UNESCO status, however, confers a level of prestige, involves national governments, ensures expert advice and guidance and gives access to extra funding. The future of these eight monuments is now secure.

They are open for visitors from all over the world to enjoy and admire. It is hoped that this book contributes to a fuller understanding of them.

Roman Emperors
(From the Fourth Century)

Diocletian and Maximian (AD 284–305)
Constantius and Galerius (305)
Constantine (initially with Galerius and Licinius) (306–337)
Constantine II (337–340)
Constans (337–350)
Constantius II (337–361)
Julian (361–363)
Jovian (363–364)
Valentinian (in the west) (364–375)
Valens (in the east) (364–378)
Gratian (in the west) (375–383) then Valentinian II (383–392)
Theodosius (initially in the east) (379–395)

Western Empire	Eastern Empire
Honorius (395–423)	Arcadius (395–408)
Valentinian III (425–455)	Theodosius II (408–450)
Petronius Maximus (455)	Marcian (450–457)
Avitus (455–456)	
Majorian (457–461)	Leo (457–474)
Libius Severus (461–465)	
Anthemius (467–472)	
Olybrius (472)	
Glycerius (473–474)	Zeno (474–491)
Julius Nepos (474–475)	
Romulus Augustulus (475–476)	
	Anastasius (491–518)
	Justin (518–527)
	Justinian (527–565)

APPENDIX II

Other Principal Figures

Aetius—Military commander who served Galla Placidia and Valentinian III, by whom he was killed.

Alaric the Goth—Leader of the Gothic tribes later known as the Visigoths, responsible for the sack of Rome in 410, when he kidnapped Galla Placidia.

Amalasuinta—Daughter of Theodoric the Ostrogoth and Regent for her son Athalaric after Theodoric's death.

Arius—Priest from Alexandria, proponent of the heresy that Christ was not of the same substance as God.

Athalaric—Grandson of Theodoric the Ostrogoth and boy king of Italy.

Athaulf—Visigoth leader who succeeded Alaric, led the Visigoths into Gaul and married Galla Placidia.

Attalus—Puppet usurper emperor created by Alaric the Goth.

Attila the Hun—Ruler of the Hunnic empire, initially with his brother Bleda, and invader of Gaul and Italy.

St Augustine—Bishop of Hippo in Africa and theologian, author of *The City of God*.

Belisarius—Military commander under Justinian, led the Byzantine reconquest of Africa and Italy.

Boethius—Roman author and scholar who held office under Theodoric the Ostrogoth but was killed by him.

Cassiodorus—Roman statesman who served under Theodoric the Ostrogoth and bequeathed state papers to posterity.

Constantius—Military commander under Honorius who married Galla Placidia, became co-emperor himself but then died.

Ecclesius—Bishop of Ravenna, founder of the church of San Vitale.

Galla Placidia—Sister of Honorius, kidnapped by the Goths, married to Athaulf, later married Constantius, was the mother of Valentian III and Regent during his minority.

Geiseric—King of the Vandals, sacked Rome in 455.

Germanus—Cousin of Justinian, married to Ostrogoth Matasuintha.

Honoria—Daughter of Galla Placidia who reportedly gave Attila the Hun a pretext to invade the Roman Empire.

Julian—Ravenna banker and silversmith who funded the construction of San Vitale, Sant'Apollinare in Classe and San Michele in Africisco.

Khusro—Sassanid king of Persia and enemy of Justinian.

Matasuintha—Daughter of Amalasuinta, married against her will to the Ostrogoth leader Witigis, and later to Germanus.

Maximian—Bishop of Ravenna, promoted to archbishop, who completed and consecrated the churches of San Vitale and Sant'Apollinare in Classe.

Narses—Armenian eunuch who became military commander under Justinian and completed the reconquest of Italy.

Neon—Bishop of Ravenna who renovated and redecorated the orthodox Catholic baptistery in Ravenna: the Neonian Baptistery.

Nestorius—Archbishop of Constantinople, proponent of the Nestorian heresy that over-emphasised the human side of Christ.

Odoacer—Barbarian military commander who rebelled against Orestes, deposed the last Western emperor (Romulus Augustulus), and became self-appointed king of Italy.

Orestes—Military commander appointed by Julius Nepos whom he deposed in favour of his own young son Romulus Augustulus.

Ricimer—Military commander of barbarian origin who became a kingmaker in the last decades of the Western Empire.

Stilicho—Military commander under Honorius who effectively ruled the Western Empire until Honorius executed him.

Theodahad—Nephew of Theodoric the Ostrogoth who became king after the death of Athalaric and had Amalasuinta killed.

Theodora—Empress of Justinian and a power in her own right.

Theodoric—Ostrogoth king who overthrew Odoacer at the instigation of Eastern Emperor Zeno and established a successful Romano-Gothic kingdom in Italy.

Totila—Formidable Ostrogoth leader who fought against the Byzantine reconquest of Italy.

Ulfilas—Missionary among the Goths who translated the Bible into a Gothic language, was ordained a bishop and converted the Goths to Arianism.

Ursicinus—Bishop of Ravenna, founder of Sant'Apollinare in Classe.

Ursus—Bishop of Ravenna, known as the founder of its cathedral and baptistery.

Wallia—Visigoth leader who agreed peace terms with Constantius and returned Galla Placidia to the Romans.

Witigis—Ostrogoth leader who succeeded and killed Theodahad but was defeated when Belisarius captured Ravenna by a ruse.

Endnotes

The full references, with date and publisher details, for the modern works cited in these endnotes are given in the Further Reading list at the end.

Chapter 1

1. Ravenna's early history as a naval port is recounted in Deborah Deliyannis's *Ravenna in Late Antiquity*, pp. 26–30.
2. For Saints Apollinaris and Vitalis, see Judith Herrin and Jinty Nelson (eds) *Ravenna: Its Role in Earlier Medieval Change and Exchange*, p. 8; Mariëtte Verhoeven's *The Early Christian Monuments of Ravenna*, pp. 56 and 73; and Deliyannis, *op. cit.*, pp. 38–39 and 223–224 (where the political significance of Vitalis's supposed paternity of the patron saints of Milan is also described).
3. The sketch map of ancient Ravenna showing the eight UNESCO sites reflects the position in the mid-sixth century when they had all been constructed. The portrayal of the coast around Classe draws on the display at the archaeological site of the old port. The map here is indicative but not precise: the sandbanks and the size and shape of the big lagoon were subject to change during this era. The plan of Ravenna is based mainly on Deliyannis, *op. cit.*, pp. 42, 107, and 202, but see also Herrin and Nelson *op. cit.*, p. 89. As explained in Chapter Five, Sant'Apollinare Nuovo only gained its present name in the ninth century.
4. The population estimate for Ravenna of 10,000 at its height comes from Deliyannis, *op. cit.*, p. 116. The many churches of early Ravenna are covered in chapters 3–6 of her book.
5. For church architecture and mosaic decoration, see John Lowden's *Early Christian and Byzantine Art*; Robin Cormack's *Byzantine Art*; Alan Doig's *Liturgy and Architecture: From the Early Church to the Middle Ages*; and Richard Reece's *The Later Roman Empire*.

Chapter 2

1. The quotes from Edward Gibbon's *The History of the Decline and Fall of the Roman Empire* (1776) come from the Preface by the Author.
2. In a 1997 journal article in *Symbolae Osloenses* (Issue 72), Peter Brown characterised the picture he had portrayed in his 1971 book, *The World of Late Antiquity*, as

involving neither catastrophe nor decay. Cited by Bryan Ward-Perkins in *The Fall of Rome and the End of Civilization*, p. 4.

3. The Walter Goffart quote comes from his *Barbarian and Romans 418–584: The Techniques of Accommodation*, p. 35.
4. For the loss of comfort, convenience and skills, see Ward-Perkins, *op. cit.*, chapters V, VI, and VII.
5. The quote from St Martin comes to us from the ancient ecclesiastical writer Sulpicius Severus.
6. The history of the early Church, covering its organisation and the role of bishops, is told in Ivor Davidson's *A Public Faith*.
7. For the Goths' desire to find a home within the Roman Empire, see (in addition to Brown, Goffart, and Ward-Perkins) Peter Heather's *The Fall of the Roman Empire* and Stephen Mitchell's *A History of the Roman Empire*.
8. For Arianism, here and in Chapter 5, see, for example, Diarmaid MacCulloch's *A History of Christianity*; Ivor Davidson, *op. cit.*; and Thomas Burns's *A History of the Ostrogoths*.

Chapter 3

1. The early history of the Roman Empire up to the reign of Caracalla (211–217) is covered by Mary Beard's *SPQR*.
2. For the third century crisis, see Adrian Goldsworthy's *The Fall of the West* and for Diocletian's resolution, see this and also Stephen Mitchell's *A History of the Roman Empire*.
3. On Constantine and Constantinople, see Goldsworthy, *op. cit.*, Mitchell, *op. cit.*, Charles Odahl's *Constantine and the Christian Empire*, John Julius Norwich's *Byzantium: The Early Centuries* and the first chapter of Judith Herrin's *Byzantium: The Surprising Life of a Medieval Empire*.
4. For Ravenna's decline in the third and fourth centuries, see Deliyannis's *Ravenna in Late Antiquity*, pp. 34–37. Diocletian's visit is mentioned in Salvatore Cosentino's journal article in *Rechtsgeschichte Legal History*, p. 54.
5. The crisis starting in 376, when two tribes of Goths sought asylum in the Roman Empire, leading up to the battle of Adrianople, is very fully covered by Peter Heather in *The Fall of the Roman Empire*, as well as in Mitchell, *op. cit.*; Goffart's *Barbarian and Romans 418–584: The Techniques of Accommodation*; and Goldsworthy, *op. cit.*
6. For Ravenna in 402 see Deliyannis, *op. cit.*; Herrin and Nelson's *Ravenna: Its Role in Earlier Medieval Change and Exchange*; and Salvatore Cosentino, *op. cit.*

Chapter 4

1. The new building in Ravenna after 402 is described in Deliyannis's *Ravenna in Late Antiquity*; Cosentino's article in *Rechtsgeschichte Legal History*; and Judith Herrin's lecture *Why Ravenna*. The establishment of the Mints is covered in Vivien Prigent's contribution to Herrin and Nelson's *Ravenna: Its Role in Earlier Medieval Change and Exchange*, p. 151.
2. For the sack of Rome see, for example, Goldsworthy's *The Fall of the West*; Heather's *The Fall of the Roman Empire*; and Mitchell's *A History of the Roman Empire*.
3. The St Jerome quotation comes from the Preface to Book 1 of *The Commentary of Ezekiel*.
4. The St Augustine quote comes from Book 2 of *The City of God* and is quoted by Heather in *The Fall of the Roman Empire*, p. 231.
5. The anecdote about Honorius and his chickens comes from Procopius's *History of the Wars* and is quoted in Goldsworthy, *op. cit.*, p. 302.

6. Galla Placidia's fate as a hostage is described in Heather, *op. cit.*, pp. 238–241, and Goldsworthy, *op. cit.*, pp. 302–306.
7. For Galla Placidia's founding of San Giovanni Evangelista following her and her children's escape from shipwreck, see Deliyannis, *op. cit.*, p. 63.
8. The scholarly controversy over the figure long believed to be St Lawrence in the Mausoleum of Galla Placidia is covered by Deliyannis, *op. cit.*, pp. 78–79.
9. For a discussion of the three sarcophagi in the Mausoleum of Galla Placidia, see Giuseppe Bovini's *Ravenna: Art and History*, pp. 19–21.
10. For the invasions by the Huns and the Vandals, see Heather, *op. cit.*; Goldsworthy, *op. cit.*; and Mitchell, *op. cit.* All three recount the episode of Honoria's correspondence with Attila.
11. The emperors who resided in Rome and Ravenna respectively are listed by Deliyannis, *op. cit.*, p. 104. See also Cosentino, *op. cit.*, p. 55.

Chapter 5

1. For the history of the Ostrogoths (and for Theodoric in particular) as well as the more general histories already cited, see Peter Heather's *The Goths*; Thomas Burns's *A History of the Ostrogoths*; and John Moorhead's *Theodoric in Italy*.
2. On the *hospitalitas* debate, see Goffart's *Barbarian and Romans 418–584: The Techniques of Accommodation* (which discusses the issue at length in relation to both Odoacer and Theodoric); Moorhead, *op. cit.*, p. 33; Heather, *op. cit.*, p. 182; and Burns, *op. cit.*, pp. 75–83 and 125.
3. The quote from the letter Cassiodorus drafted for Theodoric to send to Eastern Emperor Anastasius comes from Cassiodorus's collection of letters called the *Variae*, Book 1, Letter 1.
4. The Theodoric quote about Romans and Goths comes from Peter Brown's *The World of Late Antiquity* and, with slightly different phrasing, can be found in Moorhead, *op. cit.* p. 103; Burns, *op. cit.*, p. 106; and Heather, *op. cit.*, p. 257.
5. For the social make-up of the Romans who lived in Ravenna during the Ostrogoth period, see Cosentino's article in *Rechtsgeschichte Legal History*, p. 57.
6. Procopius's praise for Theodoric is quoted in Mitchell's *A History of the Roman Empire*, p. 216.
7. Theodoric's family tree has been drawn from the fuller Tables 3a and 3b on pp. 96–97 of Burns, *op. cit.*
8. For the religious schisms, see John Julius Norwich's *Byzantium: The Early Centuries*, pp. 146–148 and 155–156, and also Burns *op. cit.*, pp. 86–92.
9. The writing of the Ulfilas Gospels on purple parchment in silver ink is recounted in Judith Herrin's *Byzantium*, p. 65.
10. The lack of extensive remains testifying to the location of Theodoric's main palace has frustrated archaeologists. However, Deliyannis (p. 120) and others confirm that his main palace was indeed adjacent to Sant'Apollinare Nuovo.
11. For the naming of Sant'Apollinare Nuovo, see Mariëtte Verhoeven's *The Early Christian Monuments of Ravenna*, p. 65.
12. The wording for the inscription in the apse of Sant'Apollinare Nuovo is taken from *Ravenna: Eight Monuments World Heritage*, the guide produced by the Municipality of Ravenna, and can be found in Deliyannis (p. 146), where the source is given as the ninth century historian Agnellus.
13. The speculation about the portrait labelled Justinian in Sant'Apollinare Nuovo is discussed in Deliyannis, pp. 172–174.
14. For Theodoric's last years and the execution of Boethius and Symmacchus, see Burns, *op. cit.*; Moorhead, *op. cit.*; and Heather, *op. cit.*
15. For the period of Amalasuinta's regency, see Moorhead, *op. cit.*; Mitchell, *op. cit.*; and Heather, *op. cit.*

Chapter 6

1. For the history of Justinian's reign, his foreign policy, the reconquest of Italy and the Italian civil war, see J. A. S. Evans's *The Age of Justinian*; John Moorhead's *Justinian*; Jonathan Harris's *The Lost World of Byzantium*; Judith Herrin's *Byzantium*; and John Julius Norwich's *Byzantium: The Early Centuries*.
2. The Totila quote from an embassy to Justinian is cited by John Julius Norwich, *op. cit.*, p. 243.
3. The 26,000 gold *solidi* figure is given in Deliyannis's *Ravenna in Late Antiquity*, p. 224, while Peter Brown, in *Through the Eye of a Needle*, p. 500, names 60,000 *solidi* as the total donation by Julian the banker and his family for churches in Ravenna. For the bricks, see Deliyannis, *op. cit.*, p. 220.
4. Ravenna's commercial importance and its patterns of trade are covered in Judith Herrin's *Byzantium*, p. 68; Carola Jäggi's contribution to Herrin and Nelson's *Ravenna: Its Role in Earlier Medieval Change and Exchange*, p. 108; and Cosentino's article in *Rechtsgeschichte Legal History*, p. 60.
5. For 'The Three Chapters', see Evans, *op. cit.*, Chapter 4, and John Julius Norwich, *op. cit.*, Chapter 12.
6. The use of imagery in San Vitale to reassert orthodoxy against Arianism is discussed by Deliyannis, *op. cit.*, pp. 249–250.
7. Archbishop Maximian's altar cloth with images of his predecessors is mentioned by Mariëtte Verhoeven's *The Early Christian Monuments of Ravenna*, p. 20, and by Deliyannis, *op. cit.*, p. 212.
8. The list of Bishops of Ravenna and their dates comes from Deliyannis, *op. cit.*, p. 304.
9. For the wealth of the Church in Ravenna, and the imperial donations, see Cosentino, *op. cit.*, p. 59.
10. For Justinian's final years, again see the works already cited by J. A. S. Evans; John Moorhead; Jonathan Harris; and John Julius Norwich.

Chapter 7

1. For the possible influence of the church of Saints Sergius and Bacchus in Constantinople on the design of San Vitale, see Deliyannis's *Ravenna in Late Antiquity*, pp. 225–226, and Carola Jäggi's contribution to Herrin and Nelson's *Ravenna: Its Role in Earlier Medieval Change and Exchange*, p. 94.
2. Ravenna's reorientation northwards towards the Holy Roman Empire is explored in Tom Brown's contribution to Herrin and Nelson, *op. cit.*, pp. 335–344. See also Cosentino's article in *Rechtsgeschichte Legal History*, p. 63.
3. The destruction of some churches and the survival and alteration of others is covered very comprehensively in Mariëtte Verhoeven's *The Early Christian Monuments of Ravenna*, Chapters 6 and 7 and Part 3. See also Deliyannis, *op. cit.* and, for the eight UNESCO sites, Clementini Rizzardi's text in the guide produced by the Municipality of Ravenna.
4. The inscription of the eight Ravenna monuments in the UNESCO World Heritage List is also described in the Municipality of Ravenna guide.